THE THEOLOGY OF CHAPLAINCY

The Theological Foundations of Chaplaincy

Dr. Maxwell Shimba

Shimba Publishing, LLC.

Printed by Shimba Publishing LLC
Printed in the United States of America

TABLE OF CONTENTS

INTRODUCTION

The Theology of Chaplaincy

The ministry of chaplaincy occupies a unique and vital role within the broader framework of spiritual care, offering a presence that embodies the love, compassion, and guidance of God in a variety of secular and religious settings. From hospitals and prisons to military units, universities, and corporate workplaces, chaplains serve as spiritual caregivers, counselors, and advocates for individuals from diverse backgrounds and beliefs. The theology of chaplaincy, therefore, is not merely an abstract concept but a lived reality that reflects the heart of God's mission in the world.

This book, The Theology of Chaplaincy, seeks to explore the theological foundations of chaplaincy, providing a comprehensive understanding of its role, challenges, and significance in contemporary society. Through a careful examination of scriptural teachings, historical developments, and practical applications, this book will offer valuable insights for current and aspiring chaplains, theologians, and anyone interested in the intersection of faith and service.

Defining Chaplaincy

Chaplaincy is a form of ministry that transcends the traditional boundaries of parish or congregational work, operating instead within institutional settings that may not be explicitly religious. Chaplains are called to serve in places where people often face profound life challenges—whether it be in the uncertainty of a hospital room, the isolation of a prison cell, the pressures of military service, or the complexities of a corporate environment. Unlike parish ministers who primarily serve within the context of a particular faith community, chaplains minister to individuals from all walks of life, offering spiritual care that is both inclusive and respectful of diverse beliefs.

The term "chaplain" itself has its origins in the Latin word cappellanus, referring to clergy who were entrusted with the care of sacred relics, particularly the cloak of Saint Martin of Tours. Over time, the role of chaplains evolved to include providing spiritual care to soldiers, prisoners, and those in need. Today, chaplaincy has expanded far beyond its early military roots, becoming an integral part of various institutions worldwide.

The Theological Foundations of Chaplaincy

At the heart of chaplaincy is a theology that is deeply rooted in the Christian tradition, yet broad enough to encompass a wide range of spiritual needs. Central to this theology are several key principles:

- The Ministry of Presence: Chaplains embody the presence of God in places of suffering, uncertainty, and need. This concept is exemplified in the biblical image of God as a shepherd who walks with His people through the "valley of the shadow of death" (Psalm 23). The ministry of presence is not about offering easy answers or solutions but about being there—offering comfort, hope, and a listening ear.

- Serving the Marginalized: Following the example of Jesus, chaplains are called to serve those who are often overlooked or marginalized by society. Whether it is the sick, the imprisoned, or those struggling with mental health issues, chaplains reach out to offer care and support, reflecting the inclusive love of God.

- Incarnation: The incarnation of Christ—God becoming human in the person of Jesus—is a powerful model for chaplaincy. Just as Jesus entered into the human experience to bring hope and healing, chaplains enter into the lives of those they serve, offering empathy, understanding, and spiritual guidance.

- Compassion and Reconciliation: Compassion is at the core of chaplaincy, reflecting the heart of God's love for humanity. The parable of the Good Samaritan (Luke 10:25-37) illustrates the importance of showing compassion to all, regardless of their background or circumstances. Moreover, chaplains often play a crucial role in facilitating reconciliation, whether it be between individuals, families, or communities, embodying the reconciling work of Christ (2 Corinthians 5:18-19).

The Challenges and Opportunities of Chaplaincy

The practice of chaplaincy is not without its challenges. Chaplains must navigate the complexities of serving in environments where religious beliefs may be diverse or even contested. They must be adept at offering spiritual care that is sensitive to different faith traditions while remaining true to their own theological convictions. Additionally, chaplains often face ethical dilemmas, such as maintaining confidentiality, setting appropriate boundaries, and addressing the spiritual needs of those who may not share their beliefs.

Despite these challenges, chaplaincy offers unique opportunities for ministry. Chaplains have the privilege of accompanying individuals during some of the most critical moments of their lives—whether it is offering solace to a dying patient, providing counsel to a soldier struggling with trauma, or helping a student navigate the pressures of academic life. In these moments, chaplains are able to witness the transformative power of God's love and grace.

The Purpose of This Book

The Theology of Chaplaincy aims to provide a comprehensive exploration of the theological foundations, historical developments, and practical aspects of chaplaincy. By delving into the rich theological heritage that underpins chaplaincy, this book will offer insights into how chaplains can effectively minister in diverse and often challenging contexts.

Each chapter of this book will address a different aspect of chaplaincy, from its historical roots to its modern-day applications. We will explore the ethical challenges chaplains face, the importance of cultural competence, and the role of chaplains in promoting interfaith dialogue. We will also look at emerging trends in chaplaincy, such as the increasing use of technology in providing spiritual care and the growing recognition of the importance of mental health.

Ultimately, this book seeks to equip chaplains with the theological knowledge, practical skills, and spiritual wisdom they need to carry out their ministry with integrity and compassion. Whether you are a seasoned chaplain, a student of theology, or someone interested in the practice of spiritual care, The Theology of Chaplaincy offers a rich resource for understanding and engaging with this vital ministry.

As we embark on this journey, let us be reminded of the words of Jesus, who called His followers to be salt and light in the world (Matthew 5:13-16). Chaplains, in their unique role, are called to be just that—bringing the light of God's love into the darkest corners of our world and preserving the dignity and hope of all those they serve.

DR. MAXWELL SHIMBA

CHAPTER 01

WHAT IS CHAPLAINCY?

Chaplaincy is a unique ministry that provides spiritual care and support in various secular settings, such as the military, hospitals, prisons, universities, and workplaces. Unlike traditional parish ministry, chaplains work within organizations that may not have a specific religious affiliation, serving individuals from diverse backgrounds and beliefs. This distinctive role allows chaplains to meet people where they are, offering a ministry of presence and support in places where individuals may not have access to traditional religious communities.

Chaplains are trained to offer emotional and spiritual support, crisis intervention, and pastoral care, regardless of the recipient's faith tradition. This inclusivity is a hallmark of chaplaincy, emphasizing the universal aspects of compassion, empathy, and care. Chaplains must be adaptable, culturally competent, and skilled in navigating the complex dynamics of secular environments while maintaining their spiritual integrity.

Purpose of the Book

This book aims to explore the theological foundations of chaplaincy, providing a comprehensive understanding of its role, challenges, and significance in contemporary society. By examining the historical development, core theological principles, and practical aspects of chaplaincy, this book serves as a valuable resource for current and aspiring chaplains, theologians, and anyone interested in the intersection of faith and service.

The book is structured to offer both theoretical insights and practical guidance. It delves into the biblical and theological underpinnings of chaplaincy, tracing its evolution and highlighting key milestones in its development. Furthermore, it addresses the diverse contexts in which chaplains operate, outlining the specific challenges and opportunities associated with each setting.

The Importance of Chaplaincy

Chaplains play a crucial role in providing spiritual care in contexts where traditional religious support may be unavailable or impractical. Their presence in hospitals, for instance, offers comfort to patients and families facing medical crises, while military chaplains provide essential support to service members dealing with the stresses of deployment and combat. In prisons, chaplains offer hope and guidance to inmates, helping them find meaning and purpose even in the most challenging circumstances.

The importance of chaplaincy extends beyond individual care. Chaplains also contribute to the overall well-being of organizations by promoting ethical behavior, fostering a sense of community, and addressing moral and spiritual concerns. Their work supports the emotional and spiritual health of individuals and groups, contributing to a more compassionate and resilient society.

Scope of the Book

This book covers a wide range of topics related to chaplaincy, including:

- Historical Overview: A look at the origins and development of chaplaincy, from its early beginnings to its current form.

- Theological Foundations: An exploration of the biblical and theological principles that underpin chaplaincy, including themes such as incarnation, compassion, and reconciliation.

- Role and Responsibilities: A detailed examination of the core responsibilities of chaplains, including spiritual care, counseling, and leading religious services.

- Contextual Chaplaincy: An analysis of chaplaincy in various settings, such as the military, hospitals, prisons, universities, and workplaces.

- Pastoral Care and Counseling: Insights into the nature of pastoral care and the counseling techniques used by chaplains.

- Ethical Challenges: A discussion of the ethical issues faced by chaplains, including confidentiality, boundaries, and cultural competence.

- Interfaith Chaplaincy: An examination of the role of interfaith chaplains and the challenges and opportunities of providing spiritual care in a multi-faith context.

- Future Directions: A look at emerging trends in chaplaincy and the potential challenges and opportunities for the future.

Methodology

The research and analysis presented in this book are based on a combination of historical research, theological reflection, and practical experience. The author draws on a wide range of sources, including biblical texts, theological writings, case studies, and interviews with experienced chaplains. This multidisciplinary approach ensures a comprehensive and well-rounded perspective on the theology and practice of chaplaincy.

Personal Reflections

As the author of this book, I bring both academic knowledge and practical experience to the subject of chaplaincy. My journey into chaplaincy began with a deep sense of calling to serve those in need, and over the years, I have had the privilege of working in various chaplaincy settings. These experiences have given me a profound appreciation for the unique and vital role of chaplains in providing spiritual care and support.

Through this book, I hope to share the insights and lessons I have learned, offering guidance and inspiration to others who feel called to this important ministry. I believe that chaplaincy has the power to transform lives and communities, and I am excited to explore its theological foundations and practical applications in the chapters that follow.

Chaplaincy is a vital and dynamic ministry that brings spiritual care and support to a wide range of secular settings. By exploring the theological foundations and practical aspects of chaplaincy, this book aims to provide a comprehensive understanding of its role, challenges, and significance. Whether you are a current or aspiring chaplain, a theologian, or simply someone interested in the intersection of faith and service, I hope this book will offer valuable insights and inspiration for your journey.

Purpose of the Book

In a world that increasingly recognizes the importance of holistic care, chaplaincy has emerged as a vital ministry that addresses the spiritual and emotional needs of individuals in various settings. From hospitals and military bases to universities and workplaces, chaplains provide a ministry of presence and support that transcends traditional parish boundaries. This book aims to explore the theological foundations of chaplaincy, providing a comprehensive understanding of its role, challenges, and significance in contemporary society.

The Need for Theological Foundations

The practice of chaplaincy is deeply rooted in theological principles that guide and inform the work of chaplains. Understanding these foundations is essential for both current practitioners and those aspiring to enter the field. This book seeks to uncover the biblical and theological underpinnings of chaplaincy, highlighting key themes such as the ministry of presence, compassion, and reconciliation.

Ministry of Presence

At the heart of chaplaincy is the concept of the ministry of presence. This principle is rooted in the biblical narrative, where God's presence brings comfort and hope to His people. Chaplains embody this presence, offering a compassionate and non-judgmental presence to those they serve. By exploring the theological significance of presence, this book aims to deepen the reader's understanding of its transformative power in chaplaincy.

Compassion is another cornerstone of chaplaincy, reflecting the love and care of God for humanity. The ministry of Jesus is marked by acts of compassion towards the marginalized and suffering. This book examines the theological basis for compassion in chaplaincy, drawing on biblical examples and theological reflections to illustrate how chaplains can embody this essential virtue.

Reconciliation

Reconciliation is a key theme in the Christian faith, emphasizing the restoration of relationships between God and humanity, and among individuals. Chaplains often serve as agents of reconciliation, helping individuals navigate conflicts, guilt, and broken relationships. By exploring the theological foundations of reconciliation, this book provides insights into how chaplains can facilitate healing and restoration in their ministry.

Historical Development of Chaplaincy

Understanding the historical development of chaplaincy provides valuable context for its current practice.

This book traces the evolution of chaplaincy from its early beginnings to the diverse and dynamic field it is today.

Early Beginnings

The origins of chaplaincy can be traced back to the early Christian church, where clergy provided spiritual care to soldiers and prisoners. The book examines the early forms of chaplaincy, highlighting how the ministry has adapted and evolved over time.

Expansion and Formalization

The development of chaplaincy during the medieval period, including the establishment of military and hospital chaplaincy, is explored in detail. The book also discusses the formal recognition and professionalization of chaplaincy roles in the modern era, including the development of training programs and professional standards.

Role and Significance of Chaplaincy

Chaplains play a crucial role in providing spiritual care in settings where traditional religious support may be unavailable or impractical. This book delves into the multifaceted role of chaplains, examining the various contexts in which they serve and the specific challenges they face.

Diverse Contexts

Chaplains operate in a wide range of settings, each with its own unique demands and opportunities. The book explores chaplaincy in military, hospital, prison, university, and workplace settings, providing insights into the specific nature of chaplaincy in each context.

Challenges and Opportunities

The practice of chaplaincy is not without its challenges. This book addresses common challenges faced by chaplains, such as maintaining confidentiality, navigating ethical dilemmas, and managing the emotional toll of the work. At the same time, it highlights the opportunities for growth and innovation in chaplaincy, emphasizing the importance of adaptability and ongoing professional development.

Practical Aspects of Chaplaincy

In addition to exploring the theological and historical foundations of chaplaincy, this book offers practical guidance for current and aspiring chaplains. Topics covered include pastoral care and counseling, crisis intervention, and interfaith ministry.

Pastoral Care and Counseling

Effective pastoral care requires a range of skills, including active listening, empathy, and reflective questioning. The book provides practical tips and techniques for providing pastoral care and counseling, drawing on best practices and case studies from experienced chaplains.

Crisis Intervention

Crisis intervention is a critical aspect of chaplaincy, involving immediate support and stabilization in response to traumatic events. This book offers strategies for effective crisis intervention, including how to provide support in the aftermath of accidents, natural disasters, and personal crises.

Interfaith Ministry

Chaplains often serve in diverse, multi-faith environments, requiring cultural competence and sensitivity to different religious traditions. The book explores the role of interfaith chaplains, providing guidance on how to navigate religious diversity and promote interfaith dialogue.

Audience for the Book

This book is intended for a broad audience, including current chaplains, those considering a career in chaplaincy, theologians, and anyone interested in the intersection of faith and service. By providing a comprehensive understanding of the theological foundations and practical aspects of chaplaincy, this book aims to equip readers with the knowledge and skills needed to excel in this important ministry.

Current Chaplains

For current chaplains, this book offers a deeper understanding of the theological principles that underpin their work, as well as practical guidance for addressing common challenges and opportunities for professional growth.

Aspiring Chaplains

For those considering a career in chaplaincy, this book provides a comprehensive overview of the field, including the historical development, core responsibilities, and essential skills needed for effective ministry.

Theologians and Researchers

Theological scholars and researchers will find this book a valuable resource for exploring the intersection of theology and chaplaincy. By examining the biblical and theological foundations of chaplaincy, this book contributes to the broader field of practical theology and pastoral care.

General Readers

For general readers interested in understanding the role and significance of chaplaincy, this book offers an accessible and informative introduction to the field. By exploring the diverse contexts and practical aspects of chaplaincy, readers will gain a greater appreciation for this vital ministry.

The purpose of this book is to provide a comprehensive understanding of the theological foundations, historical development, and practical aspects of chaplaincy. By exploring these themes, this book aims to equip current and aspiring chaplains with the knowledge and skills needed to provide effective spiritual care and support in diverse settings. Through a combination of theological reflection, historical analysis, and practical guidance, this book serves as a valuable resource for anyone interested in the intersection of faith and service.

CHAPTER 02

HISTORICAL OVERVIEW OF CHAPLAINCY

Early Beginnings

The history of chaplaincy is rich and multifaceted, reflecting the evolving needs of society and the enduring commitment of the church to provide spiritual care in diverse settings. The origins of chaplaincy can be traced back to the early Christian church, where clergy provided spiritual care to soldiers and prisoners. This chapter delves into the early beginnings of chaplaincy, exploring its roots, development, and the pivotal role of key figures and institutions.

The Early Christian Church and Spiritual Care

In the early Christian church, spiritual care was an integral part of the community's life and mission. The church was committed to serving not only its members but also those on the margins of society, including soldiers and prisoners. This commitment was rooted in the teachings of Jesus, who emphasized compassion, service, and the importance of caring for the least of these (Matthew 25:35-40).

Ministry to Soldiers

The Roman Empire, with its vast and powerful military, provided the context for the early ministry to soldiers. As Christianity spread throughout the empire, soldiers began to convert to the faith, bringing with them unique spiritual needs. Christian clergy recognized the importance of providing spiritual care to these soldiers, who often faced moral and ethical dilemmas, the trauma of combat, and the challenges of maintaining their faith in a military environment.

One of the earliest examples of ministry to soldiers can be found in the life of Martin of Tours, a Roman soldier who converted to Christianity and later became a bishop. Martin is best known for his act of charity in sharing his cloak with a beggar, an event that symbolized his commitment to serving others. After leaving the military, Martin continued to minister to soldiers, offering spiritual guidance and support.

Ministry to Prisoners

The early Christian church also placed a strong emphasis on caring for prisoners. Imprisonment was a common experience in the Roman Empire, often used as a means of punishment and control. Early Christians, many of whom were themselves imprisoned for their faith, understood the importance of providing spiritual support to those in captivity.

The Acts of the Apostles recounts several instances of early Christian leaders, such as Paul and Silas, ministering to fellow prisoners (Acts 16:25-34). These acts of ministry not only provided comfort and hope to prisoners but also served as powerful testimonies to the transformative power of the gospel.

The Terms "Chaplain" and Saint Martin of Tours

The term "chaplain" is derived from the Latin word "cappellanus," which originally referred to clergy entrusted with the care of the sacred relics of Saint Martin of Tours. Martin, who lived in the fourth century, is a key figure in the history of chaplaincy, and his legacy has had a lasting impact on the development of this ministry.

Saint Martin of Tours

Martin of Tours was born in what is now Hungary around 316 AD. He served in the Roman army, where he gained a reputation for his piety and charity. According to tradition, while stationed in Gaul (modern-day France), Martin encountered a beggar and, moved by compassion, cut his military cloak (cappa) in half to share with the man. That night, Martin had a vision of Christ wearing the half-cloak, affirming his act of charity.

After this experience, Martin left the military and dedicated his life to Christian service. He was later ordained as a bishop and became known for his efforts to evangelize the rural areas of Gaul, establish monasteries, and care for the poor and marginalized. His cloak, preserved as a relic, became a symbol of his ministry and a source of inspiration for future chaplains.

The Cappella and Cappellani

The relic of Saint Martin's cloak, known as the "cappa," was housed in a small shrine called a "cappella." The clergy responsible for the care of this shrine and its relics were known as "cappellani," from which the term "chaplain" is derived. These early chaplains continued the legacy of Saint Martin, providing spiritual care and support to those in need.

Expansion of Chaplaincy in the Early Church

As Christianity continued to spread, the ministry of chaplaincy expanded to include various contexts and forms. The early church recognized the importance of providing spiritual care in diverse settings, and chaplains began to serve in a range of roles.

Chaplaincy in Monastic Communities

Monasticism played a significant role in the development of chaplaincy. Monastic communities, with their emphasis on prayer, service, and hospitality, became centers of spiritual care. Monks and nuns often served as chaplains, providing care to travelers, the sick, and the poor. These communities also established hospitals and hospices, further institutionalizing the ministry of chaplaincy.

Chaplaincy in Military Contexts

The ministry to soldiers continued to evolve, with chaplains becoming an integral part of military life. By the early Middle Ages, the presence of chaplains in the military was formalized, and they were often attached to specific units or military orders. These chaplains provided not only spiritual care but also moral guidance and support, helping soldiers navigate the challenges of military service.

Chaplaincy in Hospitals and Prisons

The establishment of hospitals and prisons in the early Middle Ages provided new contexts for chaplaincy. Chaplains in these settings offered spiritual care to patients and inmates, addressing their emotional and spiritual needs. The church recognized the importance of these ministries, and chaplaincy roles in hospitals and prisons became more structured and formalized.

Theological Foundations of Early Chaplaincy

The early development of chaplaincy was underpinned by several key theological principles that continue to shape the ministry today. These principles include the ministry of presence, the call to serve the marginalized, and the emphasis on compassion and reconciliation.

Ministry of Presence

The concept of the ministry of presence, which involves being with and offering support to those in need, is rooted in the biblical narrative. God's presence with His people, as depicted in passages such as Psalm 23, serves as a model for chaplaincy. Chaplains embody this presence, offering comfort and hope to those they serve.

Serving the Marginalized

The early Christian church's commitment to serving the marginalized is evident in its ministry to soldiers and prisoners. This commitment is rooted in the teachings of Jesus, who emphasized the importance of caring for the least of these (Matthew 25:35-40). Chaplains continue this mission today, providing care to individuals who may feel isolated or overlooked.

Compassion and Reconciliation

Compassion and reconciliation are central themes in the Christian faith and key principles of chaplaincy. The ministry of Jesus, marked by acts of compassion and efforts to reconcile humanity to God, provides a powerful model for chaplains. By embodying these principles, chaplains help individuals find healing and hope.

The early beginnings of chaplaincy reflect the church's commitment to providing spiritual care and support in diverse and often challenging contexts. From the ministry to soldiers and prisoners in the early Christian church to the formalization of chaplaincy roles in monastic communities, the military, hospitals, and prisons, the foundations of chaplaincy are deeply rooted in the biblical and theological principles of presence, compassion, and reconciliation.

As we continue to explore the historical development and theological foundations of chaplaincy in the chapters that follow, it is essential to remember the legacy of figures like Saint Martin of Tours and the early chaplains who paved the way for this vital ministry. Their dedication to serving others and embodying the love of Christ provides a powerful inspiration for chaplains today.

Historical Overview of Chaplaincy

Development Through the Ages

Chaplaincy, as a ministry, has evolved significantly over the centuries, reflecting the changing needs of society and the church's response to those needs. This chapter traces the development of chaplaincy from the medieval period through the modern era, highlighting key milestones and the expansion of chaplaincy into various contexts.

The Medieval Period: Chaplaincy During the Crusades

The Crusades, which began in the late 11th century, marked a significant period in the history of chaplaincy. The need for spiritual support for soldiers engaged in these religious wars led to the formal establishment of military chaplaincy.

The Role of Military Chaplains

During the Crusades, military chaplains were appointed to accompany soldiers on their campaigns. Their responsibilities included conducting religious services, administering sacraments, offering spiritual guidance, and providing moral support. The presence of chaplains on the battlefield was seen as essential for maintaining the spiritual well-being and morale of the troops.

Orders of Chaplains

The Crusades also saw the formation of military orders, such as the Knights Hospitaller and the Knights Templar, which included chaplains among their ranks. These orders combined military and religious functions, with chaplains playing a crucial role in both the spiritual and practical aspects of their missions. The Knights Hospitaller, for example, provided care for sick and wounded soldiers, establishing hospitals that would become significant sites for chaplaincy.

The Rise of Hospital Chaplaincy in Medieval Europe

The medieval period also witnessed the rise of hospital chaplaincy, as religious orders and monastic communities established hospitals to care for the sick and the poor.

Monastic Contributions

Monastic communities, such as the Benedictines and the Cistercians, played a pivotal role in the development of hospital chaplaincy. These communities founded hospitals and hospices as extensions of their commitment to service and hospitality. Monks and nuns served as chaplains, providing spiritual care, comfort, and medical assistance to patients.

Theological Foundations

The theological basis for hospital chaplaincy in medieval Europe was rooted in the Christian imperative to care for the sick and the suffering. The parable of the Good Samaritan (Luke 10:25-37) and Jesus' healing ministry provided a powerful model for this work. Hospital chaplains saw their role as an extension of Christ's compassion and healing presence.

The Reformation and the Expansion of Chaplaincy

The Reformation in the 16th century brought significant changes to the church and society, impacting the development of chaplaincy.

Protestant Chaplaincy

The Protestant Reformation led to the establishment of new forms of chaplaincy within Protestant communities. Chaplains were appointed to serve in various contexts, including universities, hospitals, and the military. Protestant chaplains emphasized the importance of preaching, pastoral care, and the administration of the sacraments.

Catholic Reformation

The Catholic Reformation, or Counter-Reformation, also saw the strengthening and expansion of chaplaincy roles within the Catholic Church. New religious orders, such as the Jesuits, played a significant role in providing spiritual care and education. Jesuit chaplains served in schools, hospitals, and mission fields, emphasizing the importance of pastoral care and spiritual formation.

The 19th Century: Formal Recognition of Prison Chaplaincy

The 19th century marked a significant period in the formal recognition and development of prison chaplaincy.

Early Efforts and Reform Movements

Efforts to provide spiritual care to prisoners can be traced back to earlier periods, but the 19th century saw a more structured and systematic approach. The rise of prison reform movements, influenced by Enlightenment ideals and Christian humanitarianism, highlighted the need for moral and spiritual rehabilitation of inmates.

Establishment of Prison Chaplaincy

Governments and religious organizations began to formally recognize the role of chaplains in prisons. Prison chaplains were tasked with providing spiritual guidance, conducting religious services, and promoting moral reform among inmates. Their work was seen as essential for the rehabilitation and reintegration of prisoners into society.

Challenges and Contributions

Prison chaplains faced significant challenges, including overcrowded and harsh prison conditions, resistance from authorities, and the diverse religious backgrounds of inmates. Despite these challenges, they made substantial contributions to the moral and spiritual well-being of prisoners, advocating for humane treatment and the reform of the penal system.

The 20th Century: Professionalization and Expansion

The 20th century witnessed the professionalization and further expansion of chaplaincy into new contexts, including healthcare, education, and the corporate sector.

Healthcare Chaplaincy

The growth of modern healthcare systems led to the formalization of healthcare chaplaincy. Chaplains became integral members of healthcare teams, providing spiritual care to patients, families, and staff. Organizations such as the Association of Professional Chaplains (APC) and the National Association of Catholic Chaplains (NACC) were established to set standards and provide certification for healthcare chaplains.

Educational Chaplaincy

Educational chaplaincy expanded significantly in the 20th century, with chaplains serving in schools, colleges, and universities. They provided pastoral care, spiritual guidance, and support for students, faculty, and staff. Educational chaplains also played a key role in promoting interfaith dialogue and understanding within academic communities.

Corporate Chaplaincy

The late 20th century saw the emergence of corporate chaplaincy, as businesses recognized the value of providing spiritual and emotional support to employees. Corporate chaplains addressed issues such as work-life balance, stress, and ethical challenges, contributing to a positive and supportive workplace culture.

Theological and Ethical Foundations in Modern Chaplaincy

The development of chaplaincy through the ages has been underpinned by evolving theological and ethical foundations.

Incarnation and Presence

The theology of incarnation, which emphasizes God becoming human in the person of Jesus, continues to be a foundational principle in chaplaincy. Chaplains embody this principle by being present with those they serve, offering empathy, compassion, and support.

Compassion and Healing

Compassion and healing remain central themes in chaplaincy. Chaplains are called to extend Christ's healing ministry, addressing not only physical but also emotional and spiritual suffering.

Ethics and Professional Standards

The professionalization of chaplaincy in the 20th century brought an increased focus on ethics and professional standards. Chaplains are guided by ethical principles such as confidentiality, respect for diversity, and maintaining professional boundaries. Organizations like the APC and the

NACC provide ethical guidelines and standards for practice, ensuring that chaplains offer care with integrity and professionalism.

The development of chaplaincy through the ages reflects the dynamic and evolving nature of this ministry. From its early beginnings in the Christian church to its expansion into diverse contexts in the modern era, chaplaincy has continually adapted to meet the spiritual and emotional needs of individuals in various settings. The key milestones in the history of chaplaincy, including the establishment of military chaplaincy during the Crusades, the rise of hospital chaplaincy in medieval Europe, and the formal recognition of prison chaplaincy in the 19th century have shaped the practice and understanding of chaplaincy today.

As chaplaincy continues to evolve, it remains grounded in the theological principles of presence, compassion, and healing, offering a vital ministry that addresses the holistic needs of those it serves. This chapter provides a historical overview of the development of chaplaincy, setting the stage for a deeper exploration of its theological foundations and practical aspects in the chapters that follow.

Modern Chaplaincy

In the modern era, chaplaincy has become an integral part of many institutions, reflecting society's recognition of the importance of holistic care. This chapter explores the evolution of modern chaplaincy, focusing on the development of professional standards and training programs, the expanded roles of chaplains, and the various contexts in which they serve today.

Professionalization of Chaplaincy

Establishment of Professional Standards

The professionalization of chaplaincy began in the early 20th century, with the establishment of organizations dedicated to setting standards and providing certification for chaplains. These organizations ensure that chaplains are well-trained and adhere to ethical guidelines in their practice.

Key Organizations

- Association of Professional Chaplains (APC): Founded in 1946, the APC is one of the leading organizations in the United States that certifies and supports professional chaplains. The APC sets standards for education, training, and ethical conduct, ensuring that chaplains provide high-quality spiritual care.

- National Association of Catholic Chaplains (NACC): Established in 1965, the NACC certifies and supports

Catholic chaplains, promoting professional standards and providing resources for ongoing education and development.

- College of Pastoral Supervision and Psychotherapy (CPSP): The CPSP offers certification for pastoral counselors, chaplains, and psychotherapists, emphasizing the integration of spiritual care with psychological support.

Training Programs

Professional chaplaincy training programs are designed to equip individuals with the skills and knowledge necessary to provide effective spiritual care. These programs typically include coursework in theology, pastoral care, counseling, ethics, and clinical pastoral education (CPE).

Clinical Pastoral Education (CPE)

CPE is a key component of chaplaincy training, involving supervised clinical practice in various settings such as hospitals, hospices, and prisons. CPE programs emphasize experiential learning, reflection, and peer support, helping chaplains develop the competencies needed for effective ministry.

Ethical Guidelines

Professional chaplains are guided by ethical principles that ensure the integrity and effectiveness of their ministry. Key ethical guidelines include:

- Confidentiality: Protecting the privacy of those they serve is paramount for chaplains.

- Respect for Diversity: Chaplains must honor and respect the diverse religious, cultural, and personal backgrounds of individuals.

- Professional Boundaries: Maintaining appropriate boundaries is essential to avoid conflicts of interest and ensure effective care.

Expanded Roles of Chaplains

In the modern era, the role of chaplains has expanded to address not only spiritual care but also emotional and psychological support, crisis intervention, and advocacy.

Spiritual Care

Providing spiritual care remains the core responsibility of chaplains. This involves offering prayer, conducting religious services, administering sacraments, and providing spiritual guidance and support.

Emotional and Psychological Support

Chaplains are trained to offer emotional and psychological support, addressing the holistic needs of individuals. This includes active listening, empathetic presence, and counseling to help individuals navigate life's challenges.

Crisis Intervention

Crisis intervention is a critical aspect of modern chaplaincy. Chaplains provide immediate support in response to traumatic events, such as accidents, natural disasters, and personal crises. Their presence helps stabilize individuals and communities, offering comfort and hope in times of distress.

Advocacy

Chaplains often serve as advocates for the needs and rights of those they serve. This involves speaking on behalf of individuals, addressing systemic issues, and promoting ethical practices within institutions. Advocacy can range from ensuring patients' rights in healthcare settings to supporting fair treatment of inmates in prisons.

Chaplaincy in Various Contexts

Modern chaplains serve in a wide range of settings, each with unique challenges and opportunities. This section explores the diverse contexts in which chaplains operate today.

Healthcare Chaplaincy

Healthcare chaplaincy is one of the most established forms of modern chaplaincy. Chaplains in healthcare settings provide spiritual care to patients, families, and staff, addressing the emotional and spiritual dimensions of illness and healing.

Hospitals

In hospitals, chaplains offer support to patients undergoing medical treatment, as well as their families. They work as part of interdisciplinary teams, contributing to holistic patient care and supporting staff in managing the emotional demands of healthcare work.

Hospices

Hospice chaplains provide end-of-life care, offering spiritual and emotional support to patients and their families. They help individuals find meaning and peace as they approach the end of life, and support families through the grieving process.

Military Chaplaincy

Military chaplaincy continues to play a vital role in providing spiritual care to service members and their families. Military chaplains offer support in various contexts, including deployment, combat zones, and bases.

Deployment and Combat Zones

Chaplains accompany troops on deployment, offering spiritual care and support in challenging and often dangerous environments. They conduct religious services, provide counseling, and help service members cope with the stresses of military life.

Bases and Installations

On military bases, chaplains provide ongoing support to service members and their families. They offer counseling, conduct religious services, and organize programs to promote spiritual resilience and well-being.

Prison Chaplaincy

Prison chaplaincy involves providing spiritual care and support to inmates, addressing their unique spiritual, emotional, and psychological needs.

Rehabilitation and Reform

Prison chaplains play a crucial role in the rehabilitation and reform of inmates. They offer spiritual guidance, facilitate religious services, and provide counseling to help inmates find purpose and hope. Chaplains also advocate for humane treatment and the reform of the penal system.

Reentry Support

Chaplains support inmates as they transition back into society, providing spiritual and practical assistance to help them reintegrate successfully. This includes connecting them with community resources, offering continued spiritual support, and advocating for their needs.

University Chaplaincy

University chaplaincy provides spiritual care and support to students, faculty, and staff in academic settings.

Student Support

University chaplains offer pastoral care and counseling to students, helping them navigate the challenges of academic life, personal development, and spiritual growth. They provide a safe space for students to explore their beliefs and values.

Interfaith Dialogue

University chaplains often promote interfaith dialogue and understanding within academic communities. They organize events, facilitate discussions, and create opportunities for students of different faiths to learn from one another and build mutual respect.

Workplace Chaplaincy

Workplace chaplaincy has emerged as a valuable resource in the corporate sector, providing spiritual and emotional support to employees.

Employee Well-being

Workplace chaplains address issues such as work-life balance, stress, and ethical challenges. They offer counseling, conduct workshops, and provide support for employees dealing with personal or professional difficulties.

Corporate Culture

Chaplains contribute to a positive corporate culture by promoting ethical behavior, fostering a sense of community, and supporting employees' holistic well-being. Their presence helps create a supportive and inclusive work environment.

The Impact of Modern Chaplaincy

The impact of modern chaplaincy is profound, touching the lives of individuals and communities in significant ways. By addressing spiritual, emotional, and psychological needs, chaplains contribute to the overall well-being of those they serve.

Holistic Care

Chaplains provide holistic care that integrates the spiritual, emotional, and psychological dimensions of well-being. This approach recognizes the interconnectedness of these aspects of human experience and promotes healing and resilience.

Community Support

Chaplains play a vital role in supporting communities, particularly in times of crisis. Their presence offers stability, comfort, and hope, helping communities navigate challenges and build resilience.

Ethical Leadership

Chaplains serve as ethical leaders within their institutions, advocating for justice, compassion, and ethical behavior. Their influence promotes a culture of integrity and respect, contributing to the overall health and effectiveness of organizations.

Modern chaplaincy has evolved into a dynamic and essential ministry that addresses the holistic needs of individuals in diverse settings. With professional standards, rigorous training programs, and a commitment to ethical conduct, chaplains provide spiritual, emotional, and psychological support, crisis intervention, and advocacy. Their expanded roles reflect the growing recognition of the importance of holistic care in contemporary society.

As we continue to explore the theological foundations and practical aspects of chaplaincy in the chapters that follow, it is essential to appreciate the profound impact of modern chaplaincy on individuals and communities. By embodying the principles of presence, compassion, and ethical leadership, chaplains offer a vital ministry that enriches and transforms the lives of those they serve.

CHAPTER 03

THEOLOGICAL FOUNDATIONS OF CHAPLAINCY

Biblical Basis for Chaplaincy

The theological foundations of chaplaincy are deeply rooted in the Bible, which provides a rich tapestry of themes and principles that guide the ministry of chaplains. This chapter explores the biblical basis for chaplaincy, focusing on key scriptural themes such as the ministry of presence, the call to serve the marginalized, and the model of Jesus as the ultimate shepherd and healer. Through an expository study with references to Strong's Concordance and comprehensive commentary, we will delve into these themes to understand how they shape and inform the practice of chaplaincy.

Ministry of Presence

The ministry of presence is a foundational concept in chaplaincy, emphasizing the importance of being with and offering support to those in need. This principle is deeply rooted in the biblical narrative.

Psalm 23: The Lord as Shepherd

One of the most poignant examples of the ministry of presence is found in Psalm 23. This psalm, attributed to David, portrays God as a shepherd who provides, guides and protects His flock.

Psalm 23:1-4 (ESV):

1. "The Lord is my shepherd; I shall not want."

2. "He makes me lie down in green pastures. He leads me beside still waters."

3. "He restores my soul. He leads me in paths of righteousness for his name's sake."

4. "Even though I walk through the valley of the shadow of death, I will fear no evil, for you are with me; your rod and your staff, they comfort me."

The key phrase here is "for you are with me" (Psalm 23:4). This expression of God's presence provides comfort and reassurance, even in the darkest times. Chaplains embody this presence, offering a comforting and stabilizing influence in the lives of those they serve.

Hebrews 13:5-6: God's Everlasting Presence

The New Testament also emphasizes God's enduring presence with His people.

Hebrews 13:5-6 (ESV):

5. "Keep your life free from love of money, and be content with what you have, for he has said, 'I will never leave you nor forsake you.'"

6. "So we can confidently say, 'The Lord is my helper; I will not fear; what can man do to me?'"

This passage reassures believers of God's constant presence and support. Chaplains, by their very presence, remind those they serve that they are not alone, reflecting God's promise to never leave nor forsake His people.

Call to Serve the Marginalized

Serving the marginalized is a core biblical mandate that underpins the ministry of chaplaincy. The Bible is replete with calls to care for the poor, the oppressed, and the outcast.

Isaiah 61:1: Proclamation of Good News

The prophet Isaiah speaks of the anointed servant who brings good news to the poor and binds up the brokenhearted.

Isaiah 61:1 (ESV):

1. "The Spirit of the Lord God is upon me, because the Lord has anointed me to bring good news to the poor; he has sent me to bind up the brokenhearted, to proclaim liberty to the captives, and the opening of the prison to those who are bound."

This verse, which Jesus Himself quotes in Luke 4:18-19, underscores the mission to serve those who are marginalized and in need. Chaplains fulfill this mission by reaching out to those who are often overlooked and providing them with spiritual and emotional support.

Matthew 25:35-40: The Least of These

Jesus' teaching in Matthew 25 provides a powerful mandate for serving the marginalized.

Matthew 25:35-40 (ESV):

35. "For I was hungry and you gave me food, I was thirsty and you gave me drink, I was a stranger and you welcomed me,"

36. "I was naked and you clothed me, I was sick and you visited me, I was in prison and you came to me."

37. "Then the righteous will answer him, saying, 'Lord, when did we see you hungry and feed you, or thirsty and give you drink?'"

38. "And when did we see you a stranger and welcome you, or naked and clothe you?"

39. "And when did we see you sick or in prison and visit you?'"

40. "And the King will answer them, 'Truly, I say to you, as you did it to one of the least of these my brothers, you did it to me.'"

This passage highlights the importance of serving the marginalized, as acts of compassion and service to them are seen as acts of service to Christ Himself. Chaplains, through their ministry, live out this call by serving those who are hungry, thirsty, sick, or imprisoned.

Jesus as the Ultimate Shepherd and Healer

Jesus is the ultimate model for chaplains, exemplifying the roles of shepherd and healer in His ministry.

John 10:11-15: The Good Shepherd

Jesus identifies Himself as the Good Shepherd who cares for His sheep.

John 10:11-15 (ESV):

11. "I am the good shepherd. The good shepherd lays down his life for the sheep."

12. "He who is a hired hand and not a shepherd, who does not own the sheep, sees the wolf coming and leaves the sheep and flees, and the wolf snatches them and scatters them."

13. "He flees because he is a hired hand and cares nothing for the sheep."

14. "I am the good shepherd. I know my own and my own know me,"

15. "just as the Father knows me and I know the Father; and I lay down my life for the sheep."

Jesus' self-identification as the Good Shepherd provides a powerful model for chaplaincy. Chaplains are called to care for those entrusted to them with the same dedication and sacrificial love that Jesus demonstrated.

Matthew 9:35-36: The Compassionate Healer

Jesus' ministry is also characterized by His compassion and healing.

Matthew 9:35-36 (ESV):

35. "And Jesus went throughout all the cities and villages, teaching in their synagogues and proclaiming the gospel of the kingdom and healing every disease and every affliction."

36. "When he saw the crowds, he had compassion for them, because they were harassed and helpless, like sheep without a shepherd."

Jesus' compassion for the crowds, who were "harassed and helpless," exemplifies the heart of chaplaincy. Chaplains are called to be compassionate healers, tending to the spiritual, emotional, and physical needs of those they serve.

Expository Study with Exhaustive Strong's Concordance

To deepen our understanding of these biblical themes, we turn to Strong's Exhaustive Concordance to explore key Hebrew and Greek terms related to chaplaincy.

Presence

- Hebrew: "Yĕshuw`ah" (Strong's H3444): This term, often translated as "salvation" or "deliverance," can also imply the presence of God as a source of safety and comfort (Psalm 27:1).

- Greek: "Parousia" (Strong's G3952): While commonly used to refer to the second coming of Christ, this term also signifies presence, particularly the comforting and empowering presence of Christ with His followers (1 Thessalonians 4:15-17).

Compassion

- Hebrew: "Racham" (Strong's H7355): This term means to have compassion or mercy, and it is frequently used to describe God's compassionate nature (Psalm 103:13).

- Greek: "Splagchnizomai" (Strong's G4697): This term means to be moved with compassion, highlighting the deep emotional response that Jesus often exhibited in His ministry (Matthew 9:36).

Healing

- Hebrew: "Rapha" (Strong's H7495): This term means to heal or to make whole, reflecting God's role as a healer (Exodus 15:26).

- Greek: "Therapeuo" (Strong's G2323): This term means to heal or to serve, and it is often used to describe Jesus' healing ministry (Matthew 4:23).

Comprehensive Commentary

Ministry of Presence

The ministry of presence, as seen in Psalm 23 and Hebrews 13, underscores the importance of being with those in need. The biblical narrative consistently highlights God's presence as a source of comfort and strength. Chaplains, by their presence, embody this divine attribute, offering solace and support to those they serve. This presence is not passive but active, involving listening, empathizing, and providing spiritual guidance.

Serving the Marginalized

Isaiah 61 and Matthew 25 present a compelling call to serve the marginalized. The anointed servant in Isaiah brings good news to the poor and liberty to the captives, reflecting the redemptive mission of God. In Matthew 25, Jesus identifies with the marginalized, teaching that acts of service to them are acts of service to Him. This identification with the marginalized is foundational for chaplaincy, as chaplains are called to reach out to those on the fringes of society with compassion and care.

Jesus as Shepherd and Healer

Jesus' portrayal as the Good Shepherd in John 10 and the compassionate healer in Matthew 9 provides a powerful model for chaplains. The Good Shepherd knows His sheep, cares for them, and sacrifices for them, illustrating the depth of pastoral care that chaplains are called to provide. Jesus' compassion for the harassed and helpless crowds demonstrates the importance of empathy and action in chaplaincy. Chaplains are called to follow this example, offering holistic care that addresses the spiritual, emotional, and physical needs of those they serve.

The biblical basis for chaplaincy is rich and multifaceted, providing a strong theological foundation for this vital ministry. Key scriptural themes such as the ministry of presence, the call to serve the marginalized, and the model of Jesus as the ultimate shepherd and healer, offer profound insights and guidance for chaplains. Through an expository study and comprehensive commentary, we have explored these themes, understanding how they shape and inform the practice of chaplaincy today. As we continue to delve into the theological foundations of chaplaincy in the chapters that follow, these biblical principles will remain central, guiding chaplains in their mission to provide compassionate and holistic care.

Theological Foundations of Chaplaincy

Ministry of Presence

The concept of the ministry of presence is central to chaplaincy, embodying the idea that being with and offering support to those in need can be a profound act of spiritual care. This chapter explores the biblical foundations, theological implications, and practical applications of the ministry of presence, illustrating how chaplains embody this vital aspect of their role.

Biblical Foundations of the Ministry of Presence

The ministry of presence is deeply rooted in the biblical narrative, where God's presence provides comfort, guidance, and reassurance to His people.

Psalm 23: The Lord as Shepherd

Psalm 23:1-4 (ESV):

1. "The Lord is my shepherd; I shall not want."

2. "He makes me lie down in green pastures. He leads me beside still waters."

3. "He restores my soul. He leads me in paths of righteousness for his name's sake."

4. "Even though I walk through the valley of the shadow of death, I will fear no evil, for you are with me; your rod and your staff, they comfort me."

Psalm 23 is one of the most well-known and beloved passages in the Bible, depicting God as a shepherd who provides and cares for His flock. The key phrase "for you are with me" (v. 4) highlights the comforting presence of God, especially in times of distress. This presence is not merely a passive accompaniment but an active source of comfort and guidance. Chaplains embody this divine presence, offering reassurance and support to those navigating difficult circumstances.

Hebrews 13:5-6: God's Everlasting Presence

Hebrews 13:5-6 (ESV):

5. "Keep your life free from love of money, and be content with what you have, for he has said, 'I will never leave you nor forsake you.'"

6. "So we can confidently say, 'The Lord is my helper; I will not fear; what can man do to me?'"

These verses from Hebrews emphasize God's promise to never leave nor forsake His people, providing a foundation for the ministry of presence. This assurance of God's constant support enables believers to face life's challenges with confidence and hope. Chaplains, by their presence, remind individuals of this divine promise, offering a tangible representation of God's unending support.

Matthew 28:20: The Great Commission

Matthew 28:20 (ESV):

20. "Teaching them to observe all that I have commanded you. And behold, I am with you always, to the end of the age."

In the Great Commission, Jesus assures His disciples of His continual presence. This promise is not limited to a specific time or place but extends "to the end of the age." Chaplains carry this assurance into their ministry, serving as agents of Christ's enduring presence in diverse and often challenging environments.

Theological Implications of the Ministry of Presence

The ministry of presence has profound theological implications, reflecting key aspects of God's nature and His relationship with humanity.

Incarnation

The doctrine of the incarnation, which teaches that God became human in the person of Jesus Christ, is foundational to the ministry of presence. In the incarnation, God entered into the human experience, sharing in our joys and sorrows. This act of divine presence is a model for chaplains, who are called to enter into the experiences of those they serve, offering empathy and support.

John 1:14 (ESV):

14. "And the Word became flesh and dwelt among us, and we have seen his glory, glory as of the only Son from the Father, full of grace and truth."

The incarnation underscores the importance of presence in ministry. Just as Jesus dwelt among humanity, chaplains are called to be present with those in their care, reflecting God's love and compassion.

Immanence

God's immanence, or His closeness to creation, is another key theological concept underpinning the ministry of presence. Unlike a distant deity, the God of the Bible is intimately involved in the lives of His people.

Psalm 139:7-10 (ESV):

7. "Where shall I go from your Spirit? Or where shall I flee from your presence?"

8. "If I ascend to heaven, you are there! If I make my bed in Sheol, you are there!"

9. "If I take the wings of the morning and dwell in the uttermost parts of the sea,"

10. "even there your hand shall lead me, and your right hand shall hold me."

This passage from Psalm 139 emphasizes that there is no place where God's presence is absent. Chaplains, by being present with those in need, reflect this divine immanence, offering a reminder of God's constant presence and care.

Practical Applications of the Ministry of Presence

The ministry of presence is a central aspect of chaplaincy, with practical applications in various settings. This section explores how chaplains can effectively embody this ministry in their work.

Active Listening

Active listening is a crucial skill for chaplains, enabling them to provide meaningful support and companionship. Active listening involves fully focusing on the speaker, understanding their message, responding thoughtfully, and remembering the content of the conversation. This practice demonstrates genuine concern and respect, helping individuals feel heard and valued.

James 1:19 (ESV):

19. "Know this, my beloved brothers: let every person be quick to hear, slow to speak, slow to anger."

This verse highlights the importance of listening, a foundational aspect of the ministry of presence. Chaplains who practice active listening embody God's attentive and compassionate presence.

Empathy and Compassion

Empathy and compassion are essential qualities for chaplains, allowing them to connect with and support those in their care. Empathy involves understanding and sharing the feelings of another, while compassion involves a deep awareness of and desire to alleviate their suffering.

Romans 12:15 (ESV):

15. "Rejoice with those who rejoice, weep with those who weep."

This verse encourages believers to share in the experiences of others, reflecting the empathetic and compassionate nature of God. Chaplains, by demonstrating empathy and compassion, offer a powerful ministry of presence that provides comfort and hope.

Physical Presence

The physical presence of a chaplain can be a source of great comfort and support, especially in times of crisis or distress. Simply being there, without necessarily speaking or doing anything, can convey a powerful message of solidarity and care.

Job 2:11-13 (ESV):

11. "Now when Job's three friends heard of all this evil that had come upon him, they came each from his own place...They made an appointment together to come to show him sympathy and comfort him."

12. "And when they saw him from a distance, they did not recognize him, and they raised their voices and wept, and they tore their robes and sprinkled dust on their heads toward heaven."

13. "And they sat with him on the ground seven days and seven nights, and no one spoke a word to him, for they saw that his suffering was very great."

Job's friends initially demonstrated the ministry of presence by simply sitting with him in silence, acknowledging his suffering. Chaplains, through their physical presence, offer a similar ministry, providing support through their willingness to simply be there.

Spiritual Practices

Chaplains can also embody the ministry of presence through various spiritual practices, such as prayer, scripture reading, and administering sacraments. These practices can provide spiritual comfort and strength, helping individuals connect with God's presence in their lives.

Philippians 4:6-7 (ESV):

6. "Do not be anxious about anything, but in everything by prayer and supplication with thanksgiving let your requests be made known to God."

7. "And the peace of God, which surpasses all understanding, will guard your hearts and your minds in Christ Jesus."

By leading individuals in prayer and other spiritual practices, chaplains help them experience God's peace and presence, providing a source of comfort and reassurance.

Challenges and Opportunities in the Ministry of Presence

The ministry of presence is not without its challenges, but it also offers significant opportunities for growth and transformation.

Emotional Toll

Providing the ministry of presence can be emotionally demanding for chaplains, as they often deal with individuals in distressing situations. It is essential for chaplains to practice self-care and seek support to maintain their emotional and spiritual well-being.

Galatians 6:2 (ESV):

2. "Bear one another's burdens, and so fulfill the law of Christ."

While bearing others' burdens is a central aspect of chaplaincy, chaplains must also recognize the importance of their own well-being to sustain their ministry.

Building Trust

Building trust with those they serve is a critical aspect of the ministry of presence. This requires time, patience, and consistency, as well as a genuine commitment to the well-being of individuals.

Proverbs 3:5 (ESV):

5. "Trust in the Lord with all your heart, and do not lean on your own understanding."

Chaplains can build trust by demonstrating reliability, integrity, and a genuine concern for the well-being of those they serve, reflecting the trustworthiness of God.

Opportunities for Transformation

The ministry of presence offers significant opportunities for transformation, both for those served and for chaplains themselves. By being present with individuals in their struggles and joys, chaplains can facilitate healing, growth, and a deeper awareness of God's presence.

2 Corinthians 1:3-4 (ESV):

3. "Blessed be the God and Father of our Lord Jesus Christ, the Father of mercies and God of all comfort,"

4. "who comforts us in all our affliction, so that we may be able to comfort those who are in any affliction, with the comfort with which we ourselves are comforted by God."

Through the ministry of presence, chaplains become conduits of God's comfort and grace, fostering transformation and hope.

The ministry of presence is a foundational aspect of chaplaincy, deeply rooted in the biblical narrative and reflecting key theological principles such as the incarnation and God's immanence. By embodying this ministry, chaplains provide a powerful source of comfort, support, and spiritual care to those in need. Through active listening, empathy, physical presence, and spiritual practices, chaplains offer a tangible representation of God's enduring presence and love. Despite the challenges, the ministry of presence offers significant opportunities for transformation, making it a vital component of effective chaplaincy. As we continue to explore the theological foundations of chaplaincy in the chapters that follow, the ministry of presence will remain central, guiding chaplains in their mission to serve and support others.

Theological Foundations of Chaplaincy

Serving the Marginalized

One of the central themes of Jesus' ministry was His focus on the marginalized and oppressed. This emphasis is evident in His interactions with lepers, sinners, and outcasts. Chaplains continue this mission by providing care to individuals who may feel isolated or overlooked within their institutional settings. This chapter explores the biblical foundations, theological implications, and practical applications of serving the marginalized, supported by an expository study with references to Strong's Concordance.

Biblical Foundations of Serving the Marginalized

The biblical narrative consistently highlights God's concern for the marginalized, underscoring the importance of serving those who are often overlooked by society.

Luke 4:18-19: The Mission of Jesus

Luke 4:18-19 (ESV):

18. "The Spirit of the Lord is upon me, because he has anointed me to proclaim good news to the poor. He has sent me to proclaim liberty to the captives and recovering of sight to the blind, to set at liberty those who are oppressed,"

19. "to proclaim the year of the Lord's favor."

In this passage, Jesus outlines His mission, which includes proclaiming good news to the poor, liberty to the captives, and setting at liberty those who are oppressed. This mission statement sets the tone for Jesus' ministry and provides a blueprint for chaplaincy. Chaplains, like Jesus, are called to serve those who are marginalized and oppressed, bringing hope and healing.

Matthew 25:35-40: The Least of These

Matthew 25:35-40 (ESV):

35. "For I was hungry and you gave me food, I was thirsty and you gave me drink, I was a stranger and you welcomed me,"

36. "I was naked and you clothed me, I was sick and you visited me, I was in prison and you came to me."

37. "Then the righteous will answer him, saying, 'Lord, when did we see you hungry and feed you, or thirsty and give you drink?'"

38. "And when did we see you a stranger and welcome you, or naked and clothe you?"

39. "And when did we see you sick or in prison and visit you?'"

40. "And the King will answer them, 'Truly, I say to you, as you did it to one of the least of these my brothers, you did it to me.'"

Jesus' teaching in Matthew 25 highlights the importance of serving the marginalized. Acts of compassion and service to the least of these are seen as acts of service to Christ Himself. This passage underscores the theological imperative for chaplains to reach out to those who are hungry, thirsty, sick, or imprisoned.

Isaiah 61:1: Proclaiming Good News

Isaiah 61:1 (ESV):

1. "The Spirit of the Lord God is upon me, because the Lord has anointed me to bring good news to the poor; he has sent me to bind up the brokenhearted, to proclaim liberty to the captives, and the opening of the prison to those who are bound."

Isaiah 61:1, which Jesus quotes in Luke 4, emphasizes the mission to bring good news to the poor and liberty to the captives. This passage reflects God's heart for the marginalized and sets a precedent for chaplains to follow in their ministry.

Theological Implications of Serving the Marginalized

Serving the marginalized has profound theological implications, reflecting core aspects of God's character and His expectations for His people.

Compassion and Justice

God's compassion and justice are central themes in the Bible, and they are closely linked to His concern for the marginalized.

Micah 6:8 (ESV):

8. "He has told you, O man, what is good; and what does the Lord require of you but to do justice, and to love kindness, and to walk humbly with your God?"

This verse encapsulates God's call to His people to act justly, love kindness, and walk humbly with Him. Serving the marginalized is a tangible expression of this call, demonstrating God's compassion and commitment to justice.

Imago Dei

The doctrine of Imago Dei, which teaches that all people are created in the image of God, underpins the call to serve the marginalized. This doctrine affirms the inherent dignity and worth of every individual, regardless of their social or economic status.

Genesis 1:27 (ESV):

27. "So God created man in his own image, in the image of God he created him; male and female he created them."

Recognizing the image of God in every person compels chaplains to treat all individuals with respect and compassion, particularly those who are marginalized.

Practical Applications of Serving the Marginalized

Chaplains serve the marginalized through various practical applications, addressing their physical, emotional, and spiritual needs.

Advocacy

Advocacy is a crucial aspect of serving the marginalized. Chaplains often find themselves in positions where they can advocate for the needs and rights of those they serve.

Proverbs 31:8-9 (ESV):

8. "Open your mouth for the mute, for the rights of all who are destitute."

9. "Open your mouth, judge righteously, defend the rights of the poor and needy."

This passage from Proverbs encourages advocacy for those who cannot speak for themselves. Chaplains can advocate within their institutions and communities to ensure that the marginalized receive fair and just treatment.

Pastoral Care

Providing pastoral care to the marginalized involves offering emotional and spiritual support, listening to their concerns, and helping them find hope and meaning in their circumstances.

James 1:27 (ESV):

27. "Religion that is pure and undefiled before God the Father is this: to visit orphans and widows in their affliction, and to keep oneself unstained from the world."

This verse highlights the importance of caring for those who are vulnerable and in need. Chaplains can offer pastoral care that addresses the unique challenges faced by the marginalized, providing a compassionate presence and spiritual guidance.

Holistic Care

Holistic care addresses the physical, emotional, and spiritual needs of individuals, recognizing the interconnectedness of these aspects of human experience.

3 John 1:2 (ESV):

2. "Beloved, I pray that all may go well with you and that you may be in good health, as it goes well with your soul."

This verse underscores the importance of holistic well-being. Chaplains can provide resources and support that address the various dimensions of health and well-being, offering a comprehensive approach to care.

Expository Study with Exhaustive Strong's Concordance

To deepen our understanding of the biblical basis for serving the marginalized, we turn to Strong's Exhaustive Concordance to explore key Hebrew and Greek terms.

Poor

- Hebrew: "Anav" (Strong's H6035): This term, often translated as "poor" or "humble," reflects those who are economically disadvantaged or oppressed (Psalm 9:18).

- Greek: "Ptochos" (Strong's G4434): This term refers to those who are economically poor and often socially marginalized (Matthew 5:3).

Oppressed

- Hebrew: "Ashuq" (Strong's H6231): This term means "oppressed" or "defrauded," highlighting those who are unjustly treated or exploited (Ecclesiastes 4:1).

- Greek: "Katadynasteuo" (Strong's G2616): This term refers to the act of oppressing or exploiting others (James 2:6).

Compassion

- Hebrew: "Racham" (Strong's H7355): This term means to have compassion or mercy, often used to describe God's compassionate nature (Psalm 103:13).

- Greek: "Splagchnizomai" (Strong's G4697): This term means to be moved with compassion, highlighting the deep emotional response that Jesus often exhibited in His ministry (Matthew 9:36).

Comprehensive Commentary

Serving the Poor and Oppressed

The biblical call to serve the poor and oppressed is clear and compelling. Throughout the Bible, God expresses His concern for those who are marginalized and commands His people to act on their behalf. The Hebrew term "Anav" (Strong's H6035) and the Greek term "Ptochos" (Strong's G4434) both reflect those who are economically disadvantaged and often socially marginalized. Chaplains, by serving the poor and oppressed, fulfill a crucial aspect of their biblical mandate.

Advocating for Justice

The call to advocate for justice is central to the ministry of serving the marginalized. The Hebrew term "Ashuq" (Strong's H6231) and the Greek term "Katadynasteuo" (Strong's G2616) both describe oppression and exploitation. Proverbs 31:8-9 and other passages emphasize the importance of speaking up for those who cannot speak for themselves. Chaplains can advocate for systemic change and individual rights, ensuring that justice is upheld for the marginalized.

Demonstrating Compassion

Compassion is a key virtue in serving the marginalized. The Hebrew term "Racham" (Strong's H7355) and the Greek term "Splagchnizomai" (Strong's G4697) both highlight the deep emotional response to the suffering of others. Jesus' compassion for the crowds in Matthew 9:36 provides a powerful model for chaplains. By demonstrating compassion, chaplains reflect God's love and care for the marginalized, offering comfort and hope.

Practical Examples of Serving the Marginalized in Chaplaincy

Hospital

Chaplaincy

In hospitals, chaplains often serve patients who are marginalized by illness or disability. They provide spiritual and emotional support, advocate for patient rights, and offer holistic care that addresses the physical, emotional, and spiritual needs of patients.

Military Chaplaincy

Military chaplains serve service members who may feel marginalized by the unique stresses of military life. They offer pastoral care, support for families, and advocacy within the military system, ensuring that the needs of service members are addressed.

Prison Chaplaincy

Prison chaplains work with inmates who are often marginalized by their incarceration. They provide spiritual guidance, emotional support, and advocacy for humane treatment and rehabilitation, helping inmates find hope and purpose.

University Chaplaincy

University chaplains serve students who may feel marginalized by academic pressures, social isolation, or personal struggles. They offer counseling, support for diverse religious and cultural backgrounds, and advocacy for student rights and well-being.

Serving the marginalized is a central aspect of chaplaincy, deeply rooted in the biblical narrative and reflecting key theological principles such as compassion and justice. By advocating for the rights of the oppressed, providing pastoral and holistic care, and demonstrating compassion, chaplains fulfill their biblical mandate to serve those who are often overlooked by society. Through an expository study with references to Strong's Concordance, we have explored the biblical foundations and practical applications of this vital aspect of chaplaincy. As we continue to delve into the theological foundations of chaplaincy in the chapters that follow, the commitment to serving the marginalized will remain a guiding principle, shaping and informing the practice of chaplaincy in diverse settings.

Theological Foundations of Chaplaincy

Theological Themes in Chaplaincy

Incarnation

The incarnation of Christ—God becoming human in the person of Jesus—provides a powerful model for chaplaincy. This theological theme underscores the importance of presence, empathy, and support in ministry. Just as Jesus entered into the human experience to bring hope and healing, chaplains enter into the lives of those they serve, embodying the love and compassion of God. This chapter explores the biblical foundations, theological implications, and practical applications of the incarnation in chaplaincy, supported by an expository study with references to Strong's Concordance.

Biblical Foundations of Incarnation

The doctrine of the incarnation is central to Christian theology, emphasizing God's willingness to enter into human history and experience.

John 1:14: The Word Became Flesh

John 1:14 (ESV):

14. "And the Word became flesh and dwelt among us, and we have seen his glory, glory as of the only Son from the Father, full of grace and truth."

This verse succinctly captures the essence of the incarnation. The Greek word for "dwelt" (σκήνωσεν, "skenoo," Strong's G4637) implies "tabernacled" or "pitched

His tent," indicating that Jesus made His home among us. This concept of God dwelling among His people is foundational for understanding the incarnational model of chaplaincy.

Philippians 2:5-8: Christ's Humility and Obedience

Philippians 2:5-8 (ESV):

5. "Have this mind among yourselves, which is yours in Christ Jesus,"

6. "who, though he was in the form of God, did not count equality with God a thing to be grasped,"

7. "but emptied himself, by taking the form of a servant, being born in the likeness of men."

8. "And being found in human form, he humbled himself by becoming obedient to the point of death, even death on a cross."

This passage emphasizes Christ's humility and willingness to enter fully into the human condition, even to the point of death. The Greek term for "emptied" (ἐκένωσεν, "kenoo," Strong's G2758) conveys the idea of self-emptying or pouring out, highlighting the sacrificial nature of the incarnation.

Theological Implications of Incarnation

The incarnation has profound theological implications for chaplaincy, emphasizing presence, empathy, and identification with those in need.

Presence

The incarnation demonstrates God's commitment to being present with His creation. This presence is not distant or detached but deeply involved and relational.

Matthew 1:23 (ESV):

23. "Behold, the virgin shall conceive and bear a son, and they shall call his name Immanuel" (which means, God with us)."

The name "Immanuel" signifies God's presence with His people. Chaplains, by their presence, reflect this divine attribute, offering a tangible reminder of God's nearness and care.

Empathy

The incarnation also underscores the importance of empathy—entering into the experiences and emotions of others.

Hebrews 4:15 (ESV):

15. "For we do not have a high priest who is unable to sympathize with our weaknesses, but one who in every respect has been tempted as we are, yet without sin."

The Greek word for "sympathize" (συμπαθέω, "sympatheo," Strong's G4834) means to suffer with or to feel compassion. Jesus' empathy, born of His own human experience, sets a powerful example for chaplains.

Identification

The incarnation involves God identifying with humanity, experiencing the full range of human life.

Isaiah 53:3 (ESV):

3. "He was despised and rejected by men; a man of sorrows, and acquainted with grief; and as one from whom men hide their faces he was despised, and we esteemed him not."

This passage from Isaiah's Servant Song highlights the suffering and identification of the Messiah with human pain and sorrow. Chaplains, in their ministry, similarly identify with the struggles and suffering of those they serve.

Practical Applications of Incarnation in Chaplaincy

Chaplains can embody the incarnational model of ministry through various practical applications, emphasizing presence, empathy, and identification with those they serve.

Active Presence

Active presence involves being fully present with individuals in their times of need, offering support and companionship.

Matthew 28:20 (ESV):

20. "Teaching them to observe all that I have commanded you. And behold, I am with you always, to the end of the age."

Jesus' promise to be with His disciples always provides a model for chaplains. By being present with those in their care, chaplains embody this promise, offering a comforting and stabilizing presence.

Empathetic Listening

Empathetic listening is a key aspect of incarnational ministry, allowing chaplains to understand and share in the experiences of others.

James 1:19 (ESV):

19. "Know this, my beloved brothers: let every person be quick to hear, slow to speak, slow to anger."

This verse underscores the importance of listening, a fundamental aspect of empathetic presence. Chaplains who practice empathetic listening provide meaningful support and validation to those they serve.

Identification with Suffering

Identification with suffering involves entering into the pain and struggles of others, offering solidarity and support.

Romans 12:15 (ESV):

15. "Rejoice with those who rejoice, weep with those who weep."

This verse encourages believers to share in the experiences of others, reflecting the empathetic and compassionate nature of God. Chaplains, by identifying with the suffering of those they serve, offer a powerful ministry of presence.

Expository Study with Exhaustive Strong's Concordance

To deepen our understanding of the incarnation, we turn to Strong's Exhaustive Concordance to explore key Greek terms related to this theme.

Incarnation

- Greek: "Sarkos" (σάρξ, Strong's G4561): This term, meaning "flesh," is used in John 1:14 to describe the Word becoming flesh. It emphasizes the physical reality of the incarnation, God taking on human form.

- Greek: "Kenoo" (κενόω, Strong's G2758): This term, meaning "to empty," is used in Philippians 2:7 to describe Christ emptying Himself. It highlights the self-sacrificial nature of the incarnation.

Presence

- Greek: "Parousia" (παρουσία, Strong's G3952): While commonly used to refer to the second coming of

Christ, this term also signifies presence, particularly the comforting and empowering presence of Christ with His followers (1 Thessalonians 4:15-17).

- Greek: "Meno" (μένω, Strong's G3306): This term, meaning "to remain" or "to abide," is used in John 15:4 to describe abiding in Christ. It emphasizes the ongoing presence and relationship with Christ.

Empathy

- Greek: "Sympatheo" (συμπαθέω, Strong's G4834): This term, meaning "to suffer with" or "to feel compassion," is used in Hebrews 4:15 to describe Jesus' ability to sympathize with our weaknesses. It underscores the empathetic nature of Jesus' ministry.

Comprehensive Commentary

Incarnational Presence

The incarnation demonstrates God's commitment to being present with His creation. The Greek term "sarkos" (Strong's G4561) emphasizes the physical reality of the Word becoming flesh, underscoring the profound nature of God's presence among humanity. Chaplains, by being present with those in need, reflect this divine presence, offering comfort and support.

Empathy and Compassion

Empathy and compassion are central to the incarnational model of ministry. The Greek term "sympatheo" (Strong's G4834) highlights Jesus' ability to empathize with our weaknesses. Chaplains, by practicing empathetic listening and sharing in the experiences of those they serve, embody this compassionate presence, providing meaningful support and validation.

Identification with Humanity

The incarnation involves God identifying with humanity, experiencing the full range of human life. The Greek term "kenoo" (Strong's G2758) conveys the idea of self-emptying, highlighting the sacrificial nature of the incarnation. Chaplains, by identifying with the struggles and suffering of those they serve, offer a powerful ministry of presence and solidarity.

Practical Examples of Incarnation in Chaplaincy

Hospital Chaplaincy

In hospitals, chaplains provide incarnational presence by being with patients and their families during times of illness and crisis. They offer empathetic listening, spiritual support, and practical assistance, reflecting God's compassionate presence.

Military Chaplaincy

Military chaplains embody the incarnational model by accompanying service members in deployment and combat zones. They provide emotional and spiritual support, share in the hardships of military life, and offer a stabilizing presence in challenging environments.

Prison Chaplaincy

Prison chaplains serve as incarnational presences in the lives of inmates, offering spiritual guidance, emotional support, and advocacy. They identify with the struggles of incarceration, providing a compassionate and non-judgmental presence.

University Chaplaincy

University chaplains offer incarnational ministry by being present with students in their academic and personal journeys. They provide counseling, support for diverse religious and cultural backgrounds, and opportunities for spiritual growth, reflecting God's abiding presence.

The doctrine of the incarnation provides a powerful model for chaplaincy, emphasizing presence, empathy, and identification with those in need. By embodying these principles, chaplains offer a ministry that reflects the love and compassion of God. Through an expository study with references to Strong's Concordance, we have explored the biblical foundations, theological implications, and practical applications of the incarnation in chaplaincy. As we continue to delve into the theological foundations of chaplaincy in the chapters that follow, the incarnational model will remain central, guiding chaplains in their mission to serve and support others.

Theological Foundations of Chaplaincy

Compassion is a central theme in chaplaincy, reflecting the heart of God's love for humanity. This theme is vividly illustrated in the parable of the Good Samaritan (Luke 10:25-37), which underscores the importance of showing compassion to all, regardless of their background or circumstances. This chapter explores the biblical foundations, theological implications, and practical applications of compassion in chaplaincy, supported by an expository study with references to Strong's Concordance.

Biblical Foundations of Compassion

The Bible is replete with passages that emphasize the importance of compassion, both in God's nature and in the conduct of His people.

The Parable of the Good Samaritan

Luke 10:25-37 (ESV):

25. "And behold, a lawyer stood up to put him to the test, saying, 'Teacher, what shall I do to inherit eternal life?'"

26. "He said to him, 'What is written in the Law? How do you read it?'"

27. "And he answered, 'You shall love the Lord your God with all your heart and with all your soul and with all your strength and with all your mind, and your neighbor as yourself.'"

28. "And he said to him, 'You have answered correctly; do this, and you will live.'"

29. "But he, desiring to justify himself, said to Jesus, 'And who is my neighbor?'"

30. "Jesus replied, 'A man was going down from Jerusalem to Jericho, and he fell among robbers, who stripped him and beat him and departed, leaving him half dead.'"

31. "Now by chance a priest was going down that road, and when he saw him he passed by on the other side."

32. "So likewise a Levite, when he came to the place and saw him, passed by on the other side."

33. "But a Samaritan, as he journeyed, came to where he was, and when he saw him, he had compassion."

34. "He went to him and bound up his wounds, pouring on oil and wine. Then he set him on his own animal and brought him to an inn and took care of him."

35. "And the next day he took out two denarii and gave them to the innkeeper, saying, 'Take care of him, and

whatever more you spend, I will repay you when I come back.'"

36. "Which of these three, do you think, proved to be a neighbor to the man who fell among the robbers?"

37. "He said, 'The one who showed him mercy.' And Jesus said to him, 'You go, and do likewise.'"

The parable of the Good Samaritan highlights the essence of compassion. The Greek word for "compassion" used in verse 33 is "σπλαγχνίζομαι" (splanchnizomai, Strong's G4697), which means to be moved in one's innermost being with pity or compassion. This term vividly describes the deep, visceral reaction of the Samaritan upon seeing the injured man, leading him to take action.

Compassion in the Life of Jesus

Jesus' ministry was marked by numerous acts of compassion, demonstrating God's love and care for humanity.

Matthew 9:36 (ESV):

36. "When he saw the crowds, he had compassion for them, because they were harassed and helpless, like sheep without a shepherd."

Mark 1:40-41 (ESV):

40. "And a leper came to him, imploring him, and kneeling said to him, 'If you will, you can make me clean.'"

41. "Moved with pity, he stretched out his hand and touched him and said to him, 'I will; be clean.'"

In these passages, the Greek word for "pity" or "compassion" is again "σπλαγχνίζομαι" (splanchnizomai, Strong's G4697), emphasizing the deep emotional response that motivated Jesus to heal and help those in need.

Theological Implications of Compassion

Compassion is not just an emotional response but a profound theological principle that reflects the nature of God and His expectations for His people.

Reflecting God's Nature

God's compassion is a central aspect of His character, and He calls His people to emulate this trait.

Psalm 103:13 (ESV):

13. "As a father shows compassion to his children, so the Lord shows compassion to those who fear him."

The Hebrew word for "compassion" here is "רָחַם" (racham, Strong's H7355), which conveys a deep, parental love and care. This verse highlights the tenderness and mercy of God, which His people are called to reflect in their interactions with others.

Compassion as a Moral Imperative

Compassion is not optional but a moral imperative for followers of Christ.

Colossians 3:12 (ESV):

12. "Put on then, as God's chosen ones, holy and beloved, compassionate hearts, kindness, humility, meekness, and patience."

The Greek word for "compassionate hearts" here is "οἰκτιρμός" (oiktirmos, Strong's G3628), which means pity or mercy. This verse underscores the expectation that believers will embody compassion as a fundamental aspect of their character and conduct.

Practical Applications of Compassion in Chaplaincy

Chaplains can manifest compassion in various practical ways, ensuring that their ministry reflects the heart of God's love for humanity.

Active Listening

One of the primary ways chaplains demonstrate compassion is through active listening, providing a safe space for individuals to share their burdens and experiences.

James 1:19 (ESV):

19. "Know this, my beloved brothers: let every person be quick to hear, slow to speak, slow to anger."

Active listening involves fully engaging with the speaker, showing empathy, and validating their feelings. This practice is foundational for building trust and providing effective support.

Practical Assistance

Compassionate ministry often involves meeting the practical needs of those in distress, much like the Good Samaritan did.

1 John 3:17-18 (ESV):

17. "But if anyone has the world's goods and sees his brother in need, yet closes his heart against him, how does God's love abide in him?"

18. "Little children, let us not love in word or talk but in deed and in truth."

Chaplains can provide practical assistance, such as arranging for resources, helping with logistics, or offering a comforting presence in times of crisis.

Emotional and Spiritual Support

Providing emotional and spiritual support is a crucial aspect of chaplaincy, helping individuals navigate their struggles with hope and resilience.

Galatians 6:2 (ESV):

2. "Bear one another's burdens, and so fulfill the law of Christ."

By offering emotional and spiritual support, chaplains help individuals feel understood and supported, fostering healing and growth.

Expository Study with Exhaustive Strong's Concordance

To deepen our understanding of compassion, we turn to Strong's Exhaustive Concordance to explore key Hebrew and Greek terms.

Compassion

- Hebrew: "Racham" (רָחַם, Strong's H7355): This term means to have compassion or mercy, often used to describe God's compassionate nature (Psalm 103:13).

- Greek: "Splanchnizomai" (σπλαγχνίζομαι, Strong's G4697): This term means to be moved with compassion, highlighting the deep emotional response that motivates action (Luke 10:33, Matthew 9:36).

- Greek: "Oiktirmos" (οἰκτιρμός, Strong's G3628): This term means pity or mercy, emphasizing a heartfelt response to the suffering of others (Colossians 3:12).

Comprehensive Commentary

Compassion as Reflecting God's Heart

The biblical concept of compassion reflects the heart of God, who is described as compassionate and merciful. The Hebrew term "racham" (Strong's H7355) conveys a deep, parental love and care, illustrating God's tender mercy toward His children. In the New Testament, the Greek term "splanchnizomai" (Strong's G4697) vividly depicts the deep, visceral response of Jesus to human suffering, motivating Him to heal and help those in need.

Compassion as a Call to Action

Compassion in the Bible is not merely an emotional response but a call to action. The parable of the Good Samaritan exemplifies this, as the Samaritan's compassion leads him to take concrete steps to care for the injured man. Similarly, Jesus' acts of healing and mercy are driven by His compassionate heart, demonstrating that true compassion involves meeting the practical and spiritual needs of others.

Practical Examples of Compassion in Chaplaincy

Hospital Chaplaincy

In hospitals, chaplains demonstrate compassion by providing emotional and spiritual support to patients and their families. This includes listening to their concerns, offering prayers, and providing comfort during difficult times.

Military Chaplaincy

Military chaplains show compassion by supporting service members and their families, particularly during deployments and in combat zones. They offer counseling, facilitate communication with loved ones, and provide a comforting presence in stressful situations.

Prison Chaplaincy

Prison chaplains embody compassion by ministering to inmates, offering spiritual guidance, and advocating for their needs. They help inmates find hope and purpose, providing a non-judgmental presence and emotional support.

University Chaplaincy

University chaplains offer compassion by supporting students in their academic and personal lives. They provide counseling, facilitate support groups, and create a welcoming environment for students from diverse backgrounds.

Compassion is a central theme in chaplaincy, reflecting the heart of God's love for humanity. By embodying compassion through active listening, practical assistance, and emotional and spiritual support, chaplains fulfill their biblical mandate to care for others. Through an expository study with references to Strong's Concordance, we have explored the biblical foundations, theological implications, and practical applications of compassion in chaplaincy. As we continue to delve into the theological foundations of chaplaincy in the chapters that follow, the commitment to compassion will remain a guiding principle, shaping and informing the practice of chaplaincy in diverse settings.

Theological Foundations of Chaplaincy

Reconciliation

Reconciliation is a key theological theme that emphasizes the restoration of broken relationships. This theme is central to the Christian faith and the ministry of chaplaincy. Chaplains often play a crucial role in facilitating reconciliation between individuals, families, and communities, embodying the reconciling work of Christ. This chapter explores the biblical foundations, theological implications, and practical applications of reconciliation in chaplaincy, supported by an expository study with references to Strong's Concordance.

Biblical Foundations of Reconciliation

The Bible provides a rich foundation for understanding reconciliation, focusing on God's initiative to restore broken relationships with humanity and the call for believers to pursue reconciliation with one another.

2 Corinthians 5:18-19: The Ministry of Reconciliation

2 Corinthians 5:18-19 (ESV):

18. "All this is from God, who through Christ reconciled us to himself and gave us the ministry of reconciliation;"

19. "that is, in Christ God was reconciling the world to himself, not counting their trespasses against them, and entrusting to us the message of reconciliation."

This passage highlights the centrality of reconciliation in the Christian message. The Greek word for "reconciliation" (καταλλαγή, katallage, Strong's G2643) refers to the restoration of a right relationship between God and humanity. Paul emphasizes that this reconciliation is initiated by God through Christ and entrusted to believers as their ministry.

Romans 5:10-11: Reconciliation Through Christ's Death

Romans 5:10-11 (ESV):

10. "For if while we were enemies we were reconciled to God by the death of his Son, much more, now that we are reconciled, shall we be saved by his life."

11. "More than that, we also rejoice in God through our Lord Jesus Christ, through whom we have now received reconciliation."

Paul underscores that reconciliation with God is made possible through the death of Jesus. The term "reconciled" (καταλλάσσω, katallasso, Strong's G2644) emphasizes the transformation from a state of enmity to one of peace and harmony with God.

Theological Implications of Reconciliation

Reconciliation has profound theological implications, reflecting God's nature and His redemptive work in the world.

God's Initiative in Reconciliation

Reconciliation begins with God's initiative. It is not humanity's efforts that restore the relationship but God's grace and action.

Colossians 1:19-20 (ESV):

19. "For in him all the fullness of God was pleased to dwell,"

20. "and through him to reconcile to himself all things, whether on earth or in heaven, making peace by the blood of his cross."

This passage emphasizes that reconciliation is God's work through Christ, who brings peace and restores all things to Himself. This divine initiative is foundational for understanding reconciliation as a gift and calling for believers.

Human Participation in Reconciliation

While reconciliation is initiated by God, believers are called to participate in this ministry, reflecting God's reconciling work in their relationships with others.

Ephesians 2:14-16 (ESV):

14. "For he himself is our peace, who has made us both one and has broken down in his flesh the dividing wall of hostility"

15. "by abolishing the law of commandments expressed in ordinances, that he might create in himself one new man in place of the two, so making peace,"

16. "and might reconcile us both to God in one body through the cross, thereby killing the hostility."

This passage highlights the role of believers in breaking down barriers and fostering peace, reflecting the unity and reconciliation brought by Christ.

Practical Applications of Reconciliation in Chaplaincy

Chaplains facilitate reconciliation in various practical ways, addressing conflicts, fostering forgiveness, and promoting peace in their communities.

Mediation and Conflict Resolution

Chaplains often mediate conflicts and facilitate reconciliation between individuals, families, and groups.

Matthew 18:15-17 (ESV):

15. "If your brother sins against you, go and tell him his fault, between you and him alone. If he listens to you, you have gained your brother."

16. "But if he does not listen, take one or two others along with you, that every charge may be established by the evidence of two or three witnesses."

17. "If he refuses to listen to them, tell it to the church. And if he refuses to listen even to the church, let him be to you as a Gentile and a tax collector."

This passage provides a framework for addressing conflicts and seeking reconciliation. Chaplains can use these principles to guide mediation efforts, promoting understanding and resolution.

Promoting Forgiveness

Forgiveness is a crucial aspect of reconciliation. Chaplains can help individuals and groups work through the process of forgiveness, facilitating healing and restoration.

Colossians 3:13 (ESV):

13. "Bearing with one another and, if one has a complaint against another, forgiving each other; as the Lord has forgiven you, so you also must forgive."

This verse highlights the importance of forgiveness in the life of believers. Chaplains can encourage and guide individuals in practicing forgiveness, reflecting the grace they have received from God.

Building Peaceful Communities

Chaplains play a vital role in building peaceful communities by fostering an environment of respect, understanding, and cooperation.

Romans 12:18 (ESV):

18. "If possible, so far as it depends on you, live peaceably with all."

This verse underscores the responsibility of believers to pursue peace. Chaplains can promote reconciliation by encouraging dialogue, understanding, and mutual respect within their communities.

Expository Study with Exhaustive Strong's Concordance

To deepen our understanding of reconciliation, we turn to Strong's Exhaustive Concordance to explore key Greek terms related to this theme.

Reconciliation

- Greek: "Katallage" (καταλλαγή, Strong's G2643): This term means reconciliation, referring to the restoration of a right relationship between God and humanity (2 Corinthians 5:18-19).

- Greek: "Katallasso" (καταλλάσσω, Strong's G2644): This term means to reconcile or to restore to favor, emphasizing the transformation from enmity to peace (Romans 5:10-11).

Peace

- Greek: "Eirene" (εἰρήνη, Strong's G1515): This term means peace, reflecting the state of harmony and wholeness that results from reconciliation (Ephesians 2:14-16).

Comprehensive Commentary

Divine Initiative and Human Response

The biblical concept of reconciliation highlights God's initiative in restoring broken relationships. The Greek term "katallage" (Strong's G2643) emphasizes that reconciliation is a divine gift, made possible through Christ. Human response to this gift involves participating in the ministry of reconciliation, breaking down barriers, and fostering peace. This dual aspect of divine initiative and human response is crucial for understanding the role of chaplains in facilitating reconciliation.

The Transformative Power of Reconciliation

Reconciliation transforms relationships, turning enmity into peace and hostility into harmony. The Greek term "katallasso" (Strong's G2644) underscores this transformative process. Theologically, reconciliation reflects the redemptive work of Christ, who reconciles all things to Himself. Practically, it involves concrete actions to restore broken relationships, promote forgiveness, and build peaceful communities.

Practical Examples of Reconciliation in Chaplaincy

Hospital Chaplaincy

In hospitals, chaplains facilitate reconciliation by helping patients and families navigate conflicts and emotional strains. They provide a compassionate presence, mediate disputes, and encourage forgiveness, fostering an environment of healing and peace.

Military Chaplaincy

Military chaplains play a crucial role in reconciliation by supporting service members dealing with relational conflicts and moral injuries. They offer counseling, facilitate dialogues, and promote forgiveness, helping service members find peace and restoration.

Prison Chaplaincy

Prison chaplains work to reconcile inmates with their victims, families, and society. They provide spiritual guidance, support restorative justice initiatives, and promote forgiveness and personal transformation, helping inmates reintegrate into the community.

University Chaplaincy

University chaplains foster reconciliation by addressing conflicts among students, faculty, and staff. They facilitate dialogues, mediate disputes, and promote a culture of respect and understanding, building a peaceful and inclusive academic community.

Reconciliation is a central theological theme that emphasizes the restoration of broken relationships. By embodying the reconciling work of Christ, chaplains play a crucial role in facilitating reconciliation between individuals, families, and communities. Through an expository study with references to Strong's Concordance, we have explored the biblical foundations, theological implications, and practical applications of reconciliation in chaplaincy. As we continue to delve into the theological foundations of chaplaincy in the chapters that follow, the commitment to reconciliation will remain a guiding principle, shaping and informing the practice of chaplaincy in diverse settings.

CHAPTER 04

THE ROLE OF THE CHAPLAIN

Core Responsibilities

Chaplains play a multifaceted role, addressing the spiritual, emotional, and practical needs of individuals in various settings. This chapter explores the core responsibilities of chaplains, including providing spiritual care, offering counseling and support, leading religious services, and advocating for the needs of those they serve. By understanding these responsibilities, we can appreciate the diverse and essential contributions of chaplains to the well-being of individuals and communities.

Providing Spiritual Care

Spiritual care is at the heart of chaplaincy, encompassing a range of activities designed to nurture the spiritual well-being of individuals.

Offering Presence and Support

One of the fundamental aspects of spiritual care is the ministry of presence. Chaplains provide a compassionate and non-judgmental presence, offering support and companionship to individuals in need.

Psalm 23:4 (ESV):

4. "Even though I walk through the valley of the shadow of death, I will fear no evil, for you are with me; your rod and your staff, they comfort me."

This verse highlights the comforting presence of God, which chaplains embody in their ministry. By being present with individuals in their times of need, chaplains offer a tangible reminder of God's love and support.

Providing Spiritual Guidance

Chaplains offer spiritual guidance, helping individuals explore and deepen their faith. This can include discussing religious beliefs, facilitating prayer and meditation, and providing resources for spiritual growth.

Proverbs 3:5-6 (ESV):

5. "Trust in the Lord with all your heart, and do not lean on your own understanding."

6. "In all your ways acknowledge him, and he will make straight your paths."

By guiding individuals in their spiritual journeys, chaplains help them find direction and meaning in their lives.

Offering Counseling and Support

Chaplains provide emotional and psychological support through counseling, helping individuals navigate life's challenges and crises.

Active Listening and Empathy

Effective counseling begins with active listening and empathy. Chaplains create a safe and supportive environment where individuals can share their thoughts and feelings.

James 1:19 (ESV):

19. "Know this, my beloved brothers: let every person be quick to hear, slow to speak, slow to anger."

By listening attentively and responding with empathy, chaplains validate individuals' experiences and emotions, fostering trust and healing.

Crisis Intervention

Chaplains often provide crisis intervention, offering immediate support and stabilization in response to traumatic events. This can include emotional support, practical assistance, and referrals to additional resources.

Psalm 46:1 (ESV):

1. "God is our refuge and strength, a very present help in trouble."

In times of crisis, chaplains act as a source of stability and comfort, helping individuals find hope and resilience.

Leading Religious Services

Chaplains lead religious services and ceremonies, providing opportunities for communal worship and spiritual expression.

Conducting Worship Services

Chaplains conduct worship services, which can include prayers, readings, hymns, and sermons. These services offer individuals a chance to connect with their faith and with one another.

Hebrews 10:24-25 (ESV):

24. "And let us consider how to stir up one another to love and good works,"

25. "not neglecting to meet together, as is the habit of some, but encouraging one another, and all the more as you see the Day drawing near."

By facilitating communal worship, chaplains help foster a sense of community and mutual encouragement.

Administering Sacraments and Rituals

Chaplains administer sacraments and rituals, such as communion, baptism, weddings, and funerals. These sacred rites provide spiritual nourishment and mark significant life events.

1 Corinthians 11:23-26 (ESV):

23. "For I received from the Lord what I also delivered to you, that the Lord Jesus on the night when he was betrayed took bread,"

24. "and when he had given thanks, he broke it, and said, 'This is my body, which is for you. Do this in remembrance of me.'"

25. "In the same way also he took the cup, after supper, saying, 'This cup is the new covenant in my blood. Do this, as often as you drink it, in remembrance of me.'"

26. "For as often as you eat this bread and drink the cup, you proclaim the Lord's death until he comes."

Administering sacraments allows chaplains to provide spiritual sustenance and mark important moments in the lives of those they serve.

Advocating for Needs

Chaplains advocate for the needs and rights of individuals, ensuring they receive appropriate care and support.

Addressing Systemic Issues

Chaplains often identify and address systemic issues within institutions that affect the well-being of individuals.

This can include advocating for policy changes, better resources, and fair treatment.

Isaiah 1:17 (ESV):

17. "Learn to do good; seek justice, correct oppression; bring justice to the fatherless, plead the widow's cause."

By advocating for justice and equity, chaplains help create more supportive and compassionate environments.

Supporting Individual Rights

Chaplains support the rights of individuals, ensuring they are treated with dignity and respect. This can include advocating for religious freedoms, access to spiritual care, and protection from discrimination.

Proverbs 31:8-9 (ESV):

8. "Open your mouth for the mute, for the rights of all who are destitute."

9. "Open your mouth, judge righteously, defend the rights of the poor and needy."

By defending individual rights, chaplains help uphold the inherent dignity of every person.

Expository Study with Exhaustive Strong's Concordance

To deepen our understanding of the core responsibilities of chaplains, we turn to Strong's Exhaustive Concordance to explore key Hebrew and Greek terms.

Spiritual Care

- Hebrew: "Ruhamah" (רֻחָמָה, Strong's H7356): This term means compassion or mercy, reflecting the compassionate care chaplains provide (Hosea 2:1).

- Greek: "Paraklesis" (παράκλησις, Strong's G3874): This term means exhortation or comfort, emphasizing the role of chaplains in providing spiritual support (2 Corinthians 1:3-4).

Counseling

- Hebrew: "Yaats" (יָעַץ, Strong's H3289): This term means to advise or counsel, reflecting the guidance chaplains offer (Proverbs 15:22).

- Greek: "Noutheteo" (νουθετέω, Strong's G3560): This term means to admonish or counsel, highlighting the counseling role of chaplains (Colossians 3:16).

Advocacy

- Hebrew: "Mishpat" (מִשְׁפָּט, Strong's H4941): This term means justice or judgment, underscoring the advocacy role of chaplains (Isaiah 1:17).

- Greek: "Dikaiosyne" (δικαιοσύνη, Strong's G1343):
This term means righteousness or justice, emphasizing the
pursuit of justice in chaplaincy (Matthew 5:6).

Comprehensive Commentary

Compassionate Care and Presence

The biblical concept of compassionate care is central
to the role of chaplains. The Hebrew term "Ruhamah"
(Strong's H7356) and the Greek term "Paraklesis" (Strong's
G3874) both highlight the importance of providing comfort
and support. Chaplains embody this compassionate care
through their ministry of presence, offering a tangible
expression of God's love and mercy.

Providing Guidance and Counsel

Chaplains offer valuable guidance and counsel,
helping individuals navigate life's challenges. The Hebrew
term "Yaats" (Strong's H3289) and the Greek term
"Noutheteo" (Strong's G3560) both emphasize the advisory
role of chaplains. By providing wise counsel and empathetic
listening, chaplains support individuals in making informed
and meaningful decisions.

Advocating for Justice and Rights

Advocacy is a crucial aspect of chaplaincy, reflecting
the biblical call to seek justice and defend the rights of the
marginalized. The Hebrew term "Mishpat" (Strong's H4941)

and the Greek term "Dikaiosyne" (Strong's G1343) both underscore the importance of justice in chaplaincy. Chaplains advocate for systemic changes and individual rights, ensuring that all individuals receive fair and compassionate treatment.

Practical Examples of Core Responsibilities in Chaplaincy

Hospital Chaplaincy

In hospitals, chaplains provide spiritual care to patients and families, offer counseling and support during crises, lead religious services, and advocate for patient rights and well-being.

Military Chaplaincy

Military chaplains support service members by providing spiritual guidance, counseling during deployment, leading worship services, and advocating for the needs of service members and their families.

Prison Chaplaincy

Prison chaplains offer spiritual care and guidance to inmates, provide counseling and support, conduct religious services, and advocate for humane treatment and rehabilitation opportunities.

University Chaplaincy

University chaplains support students' spiritual and emotional well-being, offer counseling and guidance, lead religious services and interfaith dialogues, and advocate for student rights and inclusivity.

Chaplains play a vital role in addressing the spiritual, emotional, and practical needs of individuals in various settings. By providing spiritual care, offering counseling and support, leading religious services, and advocating for the needs of those they serve, chaplains make significant contributions to the well-being of individuals and communities. Through an expository study with references to Strong's Concordance, we have explored the core responsibilities of chaplains, gaining a deeper understanding of their diverse and essential roles. As we continue to delve into the role of the chaplain in the chapters that follow, these core responsibilities will remain central, guiding and informing the practice of chaplaincy in diverse settings.

The Role of the Chaplain

Spiritual Care

Providing spiritual care is the primary responsibility of chaplains. This vital aspect of their ministry involves listening, praying, and offering guidance to individuals seeking spiritual support. Spiritual care addresses the deep, often intangible needs of the soul, offering comfort, direction, and hope. This chapter explores the biblical foundations, theological implications, and practical applications of spiritual care in chaplaincy, supported by an expository study with references to Strong's Concordance.

Biblical Foundations of Spiritual Care

The Bible offers a rich foundation for understanding and practicing spiritual care. Key passages highlight the importance of listening, praying, and offering guidance as essential components of this ministry.

Listening

Listening is a foundational aspect of spiritual care, demonstrating empathy and compassion.

James 1:19 (ESV):

19. "Know this, my beloved brothers: let every person be quick to hear, slow to speak, slow to anger."

This verse underscores the importance of being quick to listen. The Greek word for "hear" (ἀκούω, akouo, Strong's G191) emphasizes attentive listening. Chaplains, by listening carefully to those they serve, validate their experiences and offer support.

Praying

Prayer is a central component of spiritual care, providing a means of connecting with God and seeking His guidance and comfort.

Philippians 4:6-7 (ESV):

6. "Do not be anxious about anything, but in everything by prayer and supplication with thanksgiving let your requests be made known to God."

7. "And the peace of God, which surpasses all understanding, will guard your hearts and your minds in Christ Jesus."

Prayer provides a sense of peace and assurance. The Greek word for "prayer" (προσευχή, proseuche, Strong's G4335) signifies a form of worship and communication with God, emphasizing its importance in spiritual care.

Offering Guidance

Offering spiritual guidance involves helping individuals navigate their spiritual journeys, and providing wisdom and insight based on biblical principles.

Proverbs 3:5-6 (ESV):

5. "Trust in the Lord with all your heart, and do not lean on your own understanding."

6. "In all your ways acknowledge him, and he will make straight your paths."

This passage encourages trust in God and seeking His guidance. The Hebrew word for "trust" (בָּטַח, batach, Strong's H982) implies confidence and reliance on God, highlighting the importance of directing individuals to trust in God's wisdom.

Theological Implications of Spiritual Care

Spiritual care has profound theological implications, reflecting key aspects of God's relationship with humanity and His expectations for His people.

Reflecting God's Compassion

Spiritual care reflects God's compassion and concern for His people.

Psalm 103:13-14 (ESV):

13. "As a father shows compassion to his children, so the Lord shows compassion to those who fear him."

14. "For he knows our frame; he remembers that we are dust."

The Hebrew word for "compassion" (רָחַם, racham, Strong's H7355) conveys a deep, parental love and care. Chaplains, by offering compassionate spiritual care, reflect this divine attribute, providing comfort and reassurance.

Participating in God's Healing Work

Spiritual care is a means of participating in God's healing work, addressing the holistic needs of individuals.

Psalm 147:3 (ESV):

3. "He heals the brokenhearted and binds up their wounds."

The Hebrew word for "heals" (רָפָא, rapha, Strong's H7495) signifies restoration and wholeness. Chaplains, through their ministry, contribute to this healing process, offering support that addresses emotional, spiritual, and physical wounds.

Practical Applications of Spiritual Care

Chaplains provide spiritual care through various practical applications, addressing the diverse needs of those they serve.

Active Listening

Active listening involves fully engaging with the individual, showing empathy, and providing a safe space for them to express their thoughts and feelings.

Proverbs 18:13 (ESV):

13. "If one gives an answer before he hears, it is his folly and shame."

Active listening requires patience and attentiveness, allowing individuals to feel heard and understood.

Leading Prayer

Leading prayer is a vital aspect of spiritual care, offering individuals a way to connect with God and seek His guidance and comfort.

James 5:13-16 (ESV):

13. "Is anyone among you suffering? Let him pray. Is anyone cheerful? Let him sing praise."

14. "Is anyone among you sick? Let him call for the elders of the church, and let them pray over him, anointing him with oil in the name of the Lord."

15. "And the prayer of faith will save the one who is sick, and the Lord will raise him up. And if he has committed sins, he will be forgiven."

16. "Therefore, confess your sins to one another and pray for one another, that you may be healed. The prayer of a righteous person has great power as it is working."

Leading individuals in prayer provides spiritual support and helps them experience God's presence and peace.

Offering Scriptural Guidance

Offering scriptural guidance involves sharing relevant Bible passages and helping individuals understand and apply biblical principles to their lives.

Psalm 119:105 (ESV):

105. "Your word is a lamp to my feet and a light to my path."

By offering scriptural guidance, chaplains help individuals find direction and wisdom in God's Word.

Expository Study with Exhaustive Strong's Concordance

To deepen our understanding of spiritual care, we turn to Strong's Exhaustive Concordance to explore key Hebrew and Greek terms.

Listening

- Greek: "Akouo" (ἀκούω, Strong's G191): This term means to hear or listen, emphasizing attentive listening (James 1:19).

- Hebrew: "Shama" (שָׁמַע, Strong's H8085): This term means to hear or listen, highlighting the importance of listening to God and others (Deuteronomy 6:4).

Prayer

- Greek: "Proseuche" (προσευχή, Strong's G4335): This term means prayer, signifying communication with God (Philippians 4:6).

- Hebrew: "Tefillah" (תְּפִלָּה, Strong's H8605): This term means prayer, emphasizing petition and intercession (1 Samuel 1:10).

Guidance

- Hebrew: "Batach" (בָּטַח, Strong's H982): This term means to trust, highlighting reliance on God's guidance (Proverbs 3:5).

- Greek: "Hodegeo" (ὁδηγέω, Strong's G3594): This term means to guide, reflecting the role of chaplains in providing spiritual direction (John 16:13).

Comprehensive Commentary

Listening as a Compassionate Presence

The biblical concept of listening highlights the importance of being fully present with individuals. The Greek term "akouo" (Strong's G191) and the Hebrew term "shama" (Strong's H8085) both emphasize attentive and empathetic listening. Chaplains, by practicing active listening, offer a compassionate presence that validates and supports individuals in their spiritual journeys.

Prayer as Connection with God

Prayer is a central aspect of spiritual care, providing a means of connecting with God and seeking His guidance and comfort. The Greek term "proseuche" (Strong's G4335) and the Hebrew term "tefillah" (Strong's H8605) both signify communication with God. Leading individuals in prayer helps them experience God's presence and find peace in His promises.

Guidance as Spiritual Direction

Offering guidance involves helping individuals navigate their spiritual journeys, providing wisdom and insight based on biblical principles. The Hebrew term "batach" (Strong's H982) and the Greek term "hodegeo" (Strong's G3594) both highlight the importance of trusting in

God's guidance. Chaplains, by offering scriptural guidance, help individuals find direction and meaning in their lives.

Practical Examples of Spiritual Care in Chaplaincy

Hospital Chaplaincy

In hospitals, chaplains provide spiritual care by listening to patients and families, leading prayer, and offering scriptural guidance. They offer comfort and support during times of illness and crisis.

Military Chaplaincy

Military chaplains support service members by providing spiritual care during deployment and in combat zones. They listen to concerns, lead prayer services, and offer guidance based on biblical principles, helping service members find strength and hope.

Prison Chaplaincy

Prison chaplains provide spiritual care to inmates, offering a listening ear, leading prayer, and sharing scriptural guidance. They help inmates find redemption and purpose, providing a compassionate presence in a challenging environment.

University Chaplaincy

University chaplains support students by providing spiritual care through active listening, leading prayer groups, and offering scriptural guidance. They help students navigate academic and personal challenges, fostering spiritual growth and well-being.

Providing spiritual care is the primary responsibility of chaplains, involving listening, praying, and offering guidance to individuals seeking spiritual support. By addressing the deep needs of the soul, chaplains offer comfort, direction, and hope, reflecting the compassion and care of God. Through an expository study with references to Strong's Concordance, we have explored the biblical foundations, theological implications, and practical applications of spiritual care in chaplaincy. As we continue to delve into the role of the chaplain in the chapters that follow, the commitment to providing spiritual care will remain central, guiding and informing the practice of chaplaincy in diverse settings.

The Role of the Chaplain

Counseling and Support

Chaplains offer counseling and support as a core part of their ministry, addressing the emotional and psychological needs of individuals. This involves helping people navigate difficult life situations, providing crisis intervention, and offering a compassionate and supportive presence. This chapter explores the biblical foundations, theological implications, and practical applications of counseling and support in chaplaincy, supported by an expository study with references to Strong's Concordance.

Biblical Foundations of Counseling and Support

The Bible provides a solid foundation for understanding the importance of counseling and support, highlighting the value of compassion, wisdom, and empathy in helping others.

Offering Comfort

Comforting those in distress is a key aspect of counseling and support.

2 Corinthians 1:3-4 (ESV):

3. "Blessed be the God and Father of our Lord Jesus Christ, the Father of mercies and God of all comfort,"

4. "who comforts us in all our affliction, so that we may be able to comfort those who are in any affliction, with the comfort with which we ourselves are comforted by God."

The Greek word for "comfort" (παράκλησις, paraklesis, Strong's G3874) emphasizes the act of coming alongside someone to provide encouragement and support. Chaplains, by offering comfort, reflect God's compassion and care.

Providing Wise Counsel

Wise counsel is essential for helping individuals make informed and meaningful decisions.

Proverbs 15:22 (ESV):

22. "Without counsel plans fail, but with many advisers they succeed."

The Hebrew word for "counsel" (עֵצָה, etsah, Strong's H6098) signifies advice or guidance. Chaplains, by offering wise counsel, help individuals navigate complex and challenging situations.

Being Present in Times of Trouble

Being present with those in trouble is a powerful form of support.

Psalm 46:1 (ESV):

1. "God is our refuge and strength, a very present help in trouble."

The Hebrew word for "help" (עֶזְרָה, ezrah, Strong's H5833) conveys the idea of assistance and support. Chaplains, by being present in times of trouble, provide a tangible expression of God's help and strength.

Theological Implications of Counseling and Support

Counseling and support have profound theological implications, reflecting the nature of God's care for His people and His call for believers to bear one another's burdens.

Reflecting God's Compassionate Care

Providing counseling and support reflects God's compassionate care for humanity.

Psalm 34:18 (ESV):

18. "The Lord is near to the brokenhearted and saves the crushed in spirit."

The Hebrew word for "saves" (יָשַׁע, yasha, Strong's H3467) signifies deliverance and rescue. Chaplains, by offering support, reflect God's desire to heal and restore the brokenhearted.

Bearing One Another's Burdens

Believers are called to bear one another's burdens, demonstrating love and solidarity.

Galatians 6:2 (ESV):

2. "Bear one another's burdens, and so fulfill the law of Christ."

The Greek word for "burdens" (βάρος, baros, Strong's G922) refers to heavy loads or difficulties. By helping individuals carry their burdens, chaplains fulfill the law of Christ, which is grounded in love and compassion.

Practical Applications of Counseling and Support

Chaplains provide counseling and support through various practical applications, addressing the diverse needs of those they serve.

Active Listening and Empathy

Active listening and empathy are fundamental to effective counseling and support.

James 1:19 (ESV):

19. "Know this, my beloved brothers: let every person be quick to hear, slow to speak, slow to anger."

By practicing active listening, chaplains show empathy and understanding, helping individuals feel heard and valued.

Crisis Intervention

Crisis intervention involves providing immediate support and stabilization during traumatic events.

Psalm 46:1 (ESV):

1. "God is our refuge and strength, a very present help in trouble."

Chaplains, by offering crisis intervention, provide a stabilizing presence and practical assistance, helping individuals navigate acute distress.

Offering Practical Guidance

Providing practical guidance helps individuals make informed decisions and find solutions to their problems.

Proverbs 11:14 (ESV):

14. "Where there is no guidance, a people falls, but in an abundance of counselors there is safety."

Chaplains offer practical guidance, drawing on their experience and knowledge to support individuals in making wise choices.

Expository Study with Exhaustive Strong's Concordance

To deepen our understanding of counseling and support, we turn to Strong's Exhaustive Concordance to explore key Hebrew and Greek terms.

Comfort

- Greek: "Paraklesis" (παράκλησις, Strong's G3874): This term means comfort or encouragement, emphasizing the act of providing support (2 Corinthians 1:3-4).

- Hebrew: "Nacham" (נָחַם, Strong's H5162): This term means to comfort or console, highlighting the role of chaplains in offering solace (Isaiah 40:1).

Counsel

- Hebrew: "Etsah" (עֵצָה, Strong's H6098): This term means advice or counsel, reflecting the importance of wise guidance (Proverbs 15:22).

- Greek: "Bouleo" (βουλεύω, Strong's G1011): This term means to advise or plan, emphasizing the role of chaplains in providing counsel (Luke 14:31).

Support

- Hebrew: "Ezrah" (עֶזְרָה, Strong's H5833): This term means help or support, underscoring the assistance chaplains provide (Psalm 46:1).

- Greek: "Boetheia" (βοήθεια, Strong's G996): This term means help or aid, highlighting the support offered by chaplains (Hebrews 4:16).

Comprehensive Commentary

Providing Comfort and Encouragement

The biblical concept of comfort and encouragement is central to the role of chaplains. The Greek term "paraklesis" (Strong's G3874) and the Hebrew term "nacham" (Strong's H5162) both emphasize the act of providing solace and support. Chaplains, by offering comfort, reflect God's compassionate care and help individuals find hope and strength in difficult times.

Offering Wise Counsel

Wise counsel is essential for helping individuals navigate complex situations. The Hebrew term "etsah" (Strong's H6098) and the Greek term "bouleo" (Strong's G1011) both highlight the importance of providing guidance and advice. Chaplains, by offering wise counsel, support individuals in making informed and meaningful decisions.

Being a Source of Support

Being a source of support involves offering practical assistance and emotional stability. The Hebrew term "ezrah" (Strong's H5833) and the Greek term "boetheia" (Strong's G996) both underscore the importance of providing help and aid. Chaplains, by being a reliable source of support, help individuals navigate their challenges and find resilience.

Practical Examples of Counseling and Support in Chaplaincy

Hospital Chaplaincy

In hospitals, chaplains provide counseling and support to patients and their families, offering comfort, crisis intervention, and practical guidance during times of illness and stress.

Military Chaplaincy

Military chaplains support service members by providing counseling during deployment, offering crisis intervention in combat zones, and providing guidance for personal and relational issues.

Prison Chaplaincy

Prison chaplains offer counseling and support to inmates, helping them navigate the challenges of incarceration, offering crisis intervention, and providing guidance for rehabilitation and reintegration.

University Chaplaincy

University chaplains support students by offering counseling for academic and personal issues, providing crisis intervention during emergencies, and offering practical guidance for decision-making and spiritual growth.

Chaplains offer counseling and support as a core part of their ministry, addressing the emotional and psychological needs of individuals. By providing comfort, wise counsel, and practical support, chaplains help individuals navigate difficult life situations and find resilience and hope. Through an expository study with references to Strong's Concordance, we have explored the biblical foundations, theological implications, and practical applications of counseling and support in chaplaincy. As we continue to delve into the role of the chaplain in the chapters that follow, the commitment to offering counseling and support will remain central, guiding and informing the practice of chaplaincy in diverse settings.

The Role of the Chaplain

Religious Services

Leading religious services, such as worship, sacraments, and ceremonies, is a key aspect of chaplaincy. These services offer communal and individual opportunities for spiritual expression and growth, helping to foster a sense of community, provide spiritual nourishment, and mark significant life events. This chapter explores the biblical foundations, theological implications, and practical applications of religious services in chaplaincy, supported by an expository study with references to Strong's Concordance.

Biblical Foundations of Religious Services

The Bible provides a robust foundation for understanding and practicing religious services, highlighting their importance in communal worship, spiritual growth, and marking significant life events.

Worship Services

Worship services are central to the life of faith, providing a space for communal worship and spiritual nourishment.

Hebrews 10:24-25 (ESV):

24. "And let us consider how to stir up one another to love and good works,"

25. "not neglecting to meet together, as is the habit of some, but encouraging one another, and all the more as you see the Day drawing near."

The Greek word for "meet together" (ἐπισυναγωγή, episynagoge, Strong's G1997) emphasizes the gathering of believers for worship and mutual encouragement. Chaplains facilitate these gatherings, creating opportunities for communal worship and spiritual growth.

Sacraments

Sacraments are sacred rites that provide spiritual nourishment and mark significant life events, such as baptism and communion.

Matthew 28:19 (ESV):

19. "Go therefore and make disciples of all nations, baptizing them in the name of the Father and of the Son and of the Holy Spirit."

1 Corinthians 11:23-26 (ESV):

23. "For I received from the Lord what I also delivered to you, that the Lord Jesus on the night when he was betrayed took bread,"

24. "and when he had given thanks, he broke it, and said, 'This is my body, which is for you. Do this in remembrance of me.'"

25. "In the same way also he took the cup, after supper, saying, 'This cup is the new covenant in my blood. Do this, as often as you drink it, in remembrance of me.'"

26. "For as often as you eat this bread and drink the cup, you proclaim the Lord's death until he comes."

The Greek word for "baptize" (βαπτίζω, baptizo, Strong's G907) and the term for "communion" (κοινωνία, koinonia, Strong's G2842) highlight the importance of these sacraments in the Christian faith. Chaplains administer these sacred rites, providing spiritual sustenance and marking important spiritual milestones.

Biblical Foundations of Religious Services (continued)

Ceremonies

Ceremonies, such as weddings and funerals, mark significant life events and provide spiritual support and guidance.

Ecclesiastes 3:1-2 (ESV):

1. "For everything there is a season, and a time for every matter under heaven:

2. "a time to be born, and a time to die; a time to plant, and a time to pluck up what is planted;"

These verses highlight the cyclical nature of life and the importance of recognizing and honoring significant moments. The Hebrew word for "time" (עֵת, et, Strong's H6256) emphasizes the appointed seasons for various life events. Chaplains play a crucial role in leading ceremonies that honor these moments, providing spiritual support and helping individuals navigate transitions.

Theological Implications of Religious Services

Religious services have profound theological implications, reflecting the nature of worship, the importance of sacraments, and the role of ceremonies in the life of faith.

Worship as Communal and Individual Expression

Worship services provide opportunities for both communal and individual spiritual expression, fostering a sense of community and personal spiritual growth.

Psalm 95:1-2 (ESV):

1. "Oh come, let us sing to the Lord; let us make a joyful noise to the rock of our salvation!"

2. "Let us come into his presence with thanksgiving; let us make a joyful noise to him with songs of praise!"

The Hebrew word for "sing" (שִׁיר, shir, Strong's H7891) and "praise" (הָלַל, halal, Strong's H1984) underscore the importance of joyful and communal worship. Chaplains facilitate worship services that invite individuals to express their faith collectively and personally.

Sacraments as Means of Grace

Sacraments are viewed as means of grace, channels through which God imparts spiritual blessings to His people.

Romans 6:3-4 (ESV):

3. "Do you not know that all of us who have been baptized into Christ Jesus were baptized into his death?"

4. "We were buried therefore with him by baptism into death, in order that, just as Christ was raised from the dead by the glory of the Father, we too might walk in newness of life."

The Greek word for "baptized" (βαπτίζω, baptizo, Strong's G907) signifies an immersion into the life and death of Christ, symbolizing spiritual rebirth. Chaplains administer sacraments, providing opportunities for individuals to experience God's grace in profound ways.

Ceremonies as Spiritual Milestones

Ceremonies mark spiritual milestones, providing opportunities for reflection, celebration, and communal support.

John 2:1-2 (ESV):

1. "On the third day there was a wedding at Cana in Galilee, and the mother of Jesus was there."

2. "Jesus also was invited to the wedding with his disciples."

The Greek word for "wedding" (γάμος, gamos, Strong's G1062) highlights the significance of marital unions. Chaplains officiate ceremonies that celebrate and sanctify important life events, offering spiritual guidance and support.

Practical Applications of Religious Services

Chaplains provide religious services through various practical applications, addressing the diverse needs of those they serve.

Conducting Worship Services

Chaplains conduct worship services, creating opportunities for communal worship and spiritual nourishment.

Hebrews 10:24-25 (ESV):

24. "And let us consider how to stir up one another to love and good works,"

25. "not neglecting to meet together, as is the habit of some, but encouraging one another, and all the more as you see the Day drawing near."

By facilitating worship services, chaplains help foster a sense of community and mutual encouragement.

Administering Sacraments

Chaplains administer sacraments, such as baptism and communion, providing spiritual nourishment and marking significant spiritual milestones.

1 Corinthians 11:23-26 (ESV):

23. "For I received from the Lord what I also delivered to you, that the Lord Jesus on the night when he was betrayed took bread,"

24. "and when he had given thanks, he broke it, and said, 'This is my body, which is for you. Do this in remembrance of me.'"

25. "In the same way also he took the cup, after supper, saying, 'This cup is the new covenant in my blood. Do this, as often as you drink it, in remembrance of me.'"

26. "For as often as you eat this bread and drink the cup, you proclaim the Lord's death until he comes."

By administering sacraments, chaplains provide spiritual sustenance and mark important spiritual events.

Leading Ceremonies

Chaplains lead ceremonies, such as weddings and funerals, offering spiritual support and guidance during significant life events.

Ecclesiastes 3:1-2 (ESV):

1. "For everything there is a season, and a time for every matter under heaven:

2. "a time to be born, and a time to die; a time to plant, and a time to pluck up what is planted;"

By officiating ceremonies, chaplains honor significant life moments and provide spiritual support to individuals and families.

Expository Study with Exhaustive Strong's Concordance

To deepen our understanding of religious services, we turn to Strong's Exhaustive Concordance to explore key Hebrew and Greek terms.

Worship

- Greek: "Episynagoge" (ἐπισυναγωγή, Strong's G1997): This term means gathering together, emphasizing communal worship (Hebrews 10:25).

- Hebrew: "Shir" (שִׁיר, Strong's H7891): This term means to sing, highlighting the importance of joyful worship (Psalm 95:1).

Sacraments

- Greek: "Baptizo" (βαπτίζω, Strong's G907): This term means to baptize, signifying immersion and spiritual rebirth (Romans 6:3-4).

- Greek: "Koinonia" (κοινωνία, Strong's G2842): This term means communion or fellowship, emphasizing the communal aspect of sacraments (1 Corinthians 11:23-26).

Ceremonies

- Greek: "Gamos" (γάμος, Strong's G1062): This term means wedding, highlighting the significance of marital unions (John 2:1-2).

- Hebrew: "Et" (עֵת, Strong's H6256): This term means time or season, emphasizing the importance of recognizing significant life moments (Ecclesiastes 3:1-2).

Comprehensive Commentary

Worship as Communal Expression

The biblical concept of worship emphasizes communal expression and mutual encouragement. The Greek term "episynagoge" (Strong's G1997) and the Hebrew term "shir" (Strong's H7891) both highlight the importance of gathering for worship. Chaplains facilitate worship services that invite individuals to express their faith collectively and personally, fostering a sense of community and spiritual growth.

Sacraments as Channels of Grace

Sacraments are viewed as channels of grace, providing spiritual nourishment and marking significant spiritual milestones. The Greek term "baptizo" (Strong's G907) signifies immersion into the life and death of Christ, while "koinonia" (Strong's G2842) emphasizes the communal aspect of sacraments. Chaplains administer these sacred rites, offering opportunities for individuals to experience God's grace and deepen their faith.

Ceremonies as Spiritual Milestones

Ceremonies mark spiritual milestones, providing opportunities for reflection, celebration, and communal support. The Greek term "gamos" (Strong's G1062) and the Hebrew term "et" (Strong's H6256) highlight the significance of recognizing and honoring significant life moments. Chaplains officiate ceremonies that celebrate and sanctify important events, offering spiritual guidance and support.

Practical Examples of Religious Services in Chaplaincy

Hospital Chaplaincy

In hospitals, chaplains conduct worship services for patients, families, and staff, administer sacraments such as communion, and lead ceremonies like memorial services, providing spiritual support and comfort during times of illness and grief.

Military Chaplaincy

Military chaplains lead worship services for service members, administer sacraments in the field, and officiate ceremonies such as weddings and funerals, providing spiritual nourishment and support during deployment and in combat zones.

Prison Chaplaincy

Prison chaplains conduct worship services for inmates, administer sacraments such as baptism, and lead ceremonies like memorial services, offering spiritual support and fostering a sense of community within the prison environment.

University Chaplaincy

University chaplains conduct worship services for students and faculty, administer sacraments such as communion, and lead ceremonies like graduation blessings and memorial services, providing spiritual support and fostering a sense of community on campus.

Leading religious services, such as worship, sacraments, and ceremonies, is a key aspect of chaplaincy. These services offer communal and individual opportunities for spiritual expression and growth, helping to foster a sense of community, provide spiritual nourishment, and mark significant life events. Through an expository study with references to Strong's Concordance, we have explored the biblical foundations, theological implications, and practical applications of religious services in chaplaincy. As we continue to delve into the role of the chaplain in the chapters that follow, the commitment to leading religious services will remain central, guiding and informing the practice of chaplaincy in diverse settings.

The Role of the Chaplain

Skills and Qualities

Effective chaplains possess a range of skills and qualities that enable them to provide meaningful support and care to those they serve. These include empathy, active listening, cultural competence, and ethical integrity. Training programs and continuing education play a crucial role in helping chaplains develop these essential competencies. This chapter explores the key skills and qualities required for effective chaplaincy, supported by biblical foundations, theological implications, and practical applications.

Empathy

Empathy is the ability to understand and share the feelings of others. It is a fundamental quality for chaplains, allowing them to connect with and support individuals in a meaningful way.

Romans 12:15 (ESV):

15. "Rejoice with those who rejoice, weep with those who weep."

The Greek word for "weep" (κλαίω, klaio, Strong's G2799) highlights the act of sharing in the emotional experiences of others. Chaplains who demonstrate empathy are able to provide compassionate care and support.

Theological Implications of Empathy

Empathy reflects the compassionate nature of God, who understands and shares in the sufferings of His people.

Hebrews 4:15 (ESV):

15. "For we do not have a high priest who is unable to sympathize with our weaknesses, but one who in every respect has been tempted as we are, yet without sin."

The Greek word for "sympathize" (συμπαθέω, sympatheo, Strong's G4834) means to suffer with or to feel compassion. Chaplains, by demonstrating empathy, reflect the empathetic nature of Christ.

Practical Applications of Empathy

Empathy involves actively listening to and understanding the experiences and emotions of others. Chaplains can demonstrate empathy by:

- Validating the feelings and experiences of those they serve.

- Providing a non-judgmental and supportive presence.

- Offering compassionate responses that reflect an understanding of the individual's situation.

Active Listening

Active listening is a crucial skill for chaplains, enabling them to fully engage with and understand the needs of those they serve.

James 1:19 (ESV):

19. "Know this, my beloved brothers: let every person be quick to hear, slow to speak, slow to anger."

The Greek word for "hear" (ἀκούω, akouo, Strong's G191) emphasizes attentive listening. Chaplains who practice active listening are able to build trust and provide effective support.

Theological Implications of Active Listening

Active listening reflects the attentiveness of God, who listens to the prayers and concerns of His people.

Psalm 34:15 (ESV):

15. "The eyes of the Lord are toward the righteous and his ears toward their cry."

The Hebrew word for "ears" (אֹזֶן, ozen, Strong's H241) signifies God's attentiveness. Chaplains, by practicing active listening, reflect the attentive nature of God.

Practical Applications of Active Listening

Active listening involves fully engaging with the speaker, demonstrating empathy, and responding thoughtfully. Chaplains can practice active listening by:

- Focusing entirely on the speaker, avoiding distractions.

- Using verbal and non-verbal cues to show attentiveness.

- Reflecting back what the speaker has said to ensure understanding.

Cultural Competence

Cultural competence is the ability to understand, respect, and effectively interact with individuals from diverse cultural backgrounds. It is essential for chaplains, who often serve in multicultural environments.

1 Corinthians 9:22 (ESV):

22. "To the weak I became weak, that I might win the weak. I have become all things to all people, that by all means I might save some."

The Greek word for "all things" (πᾶς, pas, Strong's G3956) emphasizes the inclusive approach Paul took to connect with diverse groups. Chaplains who demonstrate cultural competence are able to provide respectful and effective care.

Theological Implications of Cultural Competence

Cultural competence reflects the inclusive nature of the Gospel, which is for all people, regardless of their cultural background.

Galatians 3:28 (ESV):

28. "There is neither Jew nor Greek, there is neither slave nor free, there is no male and female, for you are all one in Christ Jesus."

The Greek word for "one" (εἷς, heis, Strong's G1520) emphasizes unity in Christ. Chaplains, by demonstrating cultural competence, reflect the inclusive nature of the Gospel.

Practical Applications of Cultural Competence

Cultural competence involves understanding and respecting cultural differences, and adapting care to meet the needs of diverse individuals. Chaplains can demonstrate cultural competence by:

- Educating themselves about different cultural practices and beliefs.

- Showing respect for cultural differences and avoiding assumptions.

- Adapting their approach to care to be culturally sensitive and appropriate.

Ethical Integrity

Ethical integrity is essential for chaplains, who must adhere to high ethical standards in their practice.

Proverbs 11:3 (ESV):

3. "The integrity of the upright guides them, but the crookedness of the treacherous destroys them."

The Hebrew word for "integrity" (תֹּם, tom, Strong's H8537) signifies uprightness and moral soundness. Chaplains who demonstrate ethical integrity are trusted and respected by those they serve.

Theological Implications of Ethical Integrity

Ethical integrity reflects the moral character of God, who is just and righteous in all His ways.

Psalm 25:21 (ESV):

21. "May integrity and uprightness preserve me, for I wait for you."

The Hebrew word for "integrity" (תם, tom, Strong's H8537) highlights the importance of moral soundness. Chaplains, by demonstrating ethical integrity, reflect the moral character of God.

Practical Applications of Ethical Integrity

Ethical integrity involves adhering to professional ethical standards and demonstrating moral soundness in all interactions. Chaplains can demonstrate ethical integrity by:

- Maintaining confidentiality and respecting the privacy of those they serve.

- Acting with honesty and transparency in all interactions.

- Adhering to professional codes of ethics and seeking guidance when ethical dilemmas arise.

Training and Continuing Education

Training programs and continuing education are essential for chaplains to develop and maintain the skills and qualities necessary for effective ministry.

Importance of Training

Training provides chaplains with the foundational knowledge and skills required for their role. This includes:

- Theological education and spiritual formation.

- Training in counseling techniques and crisis intervention.

- Education in cultural competence and ethical standards.

2 Timothy 2:15 (ESV):

15. "Do your best to present yourself to God as one approved, a worker who has no need to be ashamed, rightly handling the word of truth."

The Greek word for "approved" (δόκιμος, dokimos, Strong's G1384) emphasizes the importance of being prepared and competent. Chaplains who undergo thorough training are well-equipped to serve effectively.

Continuing Education

Continuing education ensures that chaplains remain current with best practices and continue to develop their skills. This includes:

- Participating in workshops and seminars.

- Engaging in professional development opportunities.

- Seeking supervision and mentorship to enhance their practice.

Proverbs 9:9 (ESV):

9. "Give instruction to a wise man, and he will be still wiser; teach a righteous man, and he will increase in learning."

The Hebrew word for "instruction" (תַּחְבֻּלוֹת, tachbuloth, Strong's H8458) highlights the importance of ongoing learning. Chaplains who engage in continuing education are able to provide the highest quality of care.

Practical Examples of Skills and Qualities in Chaplaincy

Hospital Chaplaincy

In hospitals, chaplains use empathy and active listening to support patients and families, demonstrate cultural competence in diverse healthcare settings, and maintain ethical integrity in all interactions.

Military Chaplaincy

Military chaplains provide counseling and support to service members, practice cultural competence in multinational environments, and uphold ethical standards in challenging situations.

Prison Chaplaincy

Prison chaplains offer empathetic care and active listening to inmates, respect cultural and religious diversity, and adhere to ethical guidelines in their ministry.

University Chaplaincy

University chaplains support students with empathy and active listening, demonstrate cultural competence in diverse campus settings, and maintain ethical integrity in all interactions.

Effective chaplains possess a range of skills and qualities, including empathy, active listening, cultural competence, and ethical integrity. These competencies enable chaplains to provide meaningful support and care to those they serve. Training programs and continuing education play a crucial role in helping chaplains develop and maintain these essential skills. Through an exploration of biblical foundations, theological implications, and practical applications, we have gained a deeper understanding of the skills and qualities required for effective chaplaincy. As we continue to delve into the role of the chaplain in the chapters that follow, the commitment to developing and demonstrating these skills and qualities will remain central, guiding and informing the practice of chaplaincy in diverse settings.

CHAPTER 05

CHAPLAINCY IN DIFFERENT CONTEXTS

Military Chaplaincy

Military chaplaincy involves providing spiritual and emotional support to service members and their families, addressing the unique challenges of military life, and promoting resilience and well-being. Military chaplains serve in various capacities, offering guidance, conducting religious services, and supporting individuals in times of crisis. This chapter explores the roles and responsibilities of military chaplains, the unique challenges they face, and the impact of their work on service members and their families.

Roles and Responsibilities of Military Chaplains

Military chaplains fulfill a range of roles and responsibilities, providing comprehensive spiritual care and support to those they serve.

Spiritual Support

Military chaplains offer spiritual support to service members, helping them navigate the complexities of military life and maintain their faith.

Psalm 91:1-2 (ESV):

1. "He who dwells in the shelter of the Most High will abide in the shadow of the Almighty."

2. "I will say to the Lord, 'My refuge and my fortress, my God, in whom I trust.'"

Chaplains provide a sense of refuge and spiritual guidance, helping service members find comfort and strength in their faith.

Counseling and Emotional Support

Chaplains offer counseling and emotional support, addressing the mental health and emotional needs of service members.

Proverbs 12:25 (ESV):

25. "Anxiety in a man's heart weighs him down, but a good word makes him glad."

By offering a listening ear and compassionate support, chaplains help alleviate the emotional burdens that service members may carry.

Conducting Religious Services

Chaplains conduct religious services, including worship, sacraments, and ceremonies, providing opportunities for spiritual expression and growth.

Matthew 18:20 (ESV):

20. "For where two or three are gathered in my name, there am I among them."

By facilitating communal worship, chaplains help foster a sense of community and spiritual connection among service members.

Crisis Intervention

Chaplains provide crisis intervention, offering immediate support during times of trauma and crisis.

Psalm 46:1 (ESV):

1. "God is our refuge and strength, a very present help in trouble."

Chaplains act as a stabilizing presence, providing practical assistance and emotional support during critical moments.

Advocacy and Support for Families

Chaplains advocate for the needs of service members and their families, ensuring they receive the support and resources they need.

Isaiah 1:17 (ESV):

17. "Learn to do good; seek justice, correct oppression; bring justice to the fatherless, plead the widow's cause."

Chaplains help address the unique challenges faced by military families, advocating for their well-being and providing support.

Unique Challenges of Military Chaplaincy

Military chaplains face unique challenges as they serve in diverse and often demanding environments.

Deployment and Combat Zones

Serving in deployment and combat zones presents significant challenges, including the physical dangers and emotional stresses of war.

Joshua 1:9 (ESV):

9. "Have I not commanded you? Be strong and courageous. Do not be frightened, and do not be dismayed, for the Lord your God is with you wherever you go."

Chaplains provide spiritual and emotional support, helping service members cope with the stresses and dangers of deployment.

Separation from Family

Separation from family during deployment can be a significant source of stress and emotional strain for service members.

Psalm 121:8 (ESV):

8. "The Lord will keep your going out and your coming in from this time forth and forevermore."

Chaplains offer support and encouragement, helping service members stay connected with their families and maintain their emotional well-being.

Moral and Ethical Dilemmas

Service members may face moral and ethical dilemmas in the course of their duties, requiring guidance and support.

Micah 6:8 (ESV):

8. "He has told you, O man, what is good; and what does the Lord require of you but to do justice, and to love kindness, and to walk humbly with your God?"

Chaplains provide counsel and support, helping service members navigate complex moral and ethical issues with integrity.

Impact of Military Chaplaincy on Service Members and Families

Military chaplaincy has a profound impact on the well-being and resilience of service members and their families.

Promoting Resilience

Chaplains promote resilience by providing spiritual and emotional support, helping service members develop coping strategies and maintain their mental health.

Philippians 4:13 (ESV):

13. "I can do all things through him who strengthens me."

By fostering a sense of spiritual strength and resilience, chaplains help service members navigate the challenges of military life.

Enhancing Well-Being

Chaplains enhance the overall well-being of service members and their families by providing comprehensive support and resources.

3 John 1:2 (ESV):

2. "Beloved, I pray that all may go well with you and that you may be in good health, as it goes well with your soul."

Chaplains address the holistic needs of service members, promoting physical, emotional, and spiritual well-being.

Fostering Community and Connection

Chaplains help foster a sense of community and connection among service members, creating opportunities for fellowship and mutual support.

Hebrews 10:24-25 (ESV):

24. "And let us consider how to stir up one another to love and good works,"

25. "not neglecting to meet together, as is the habit of some, but encouraging one another, and all the more as you see the Day drawing near."

By facilitating communal activities and worship, chaplains help service members build supportive relationships and a sense of belonging.

Practical Examples of Military Chaplaincy

Worship Services in the Field

Military chaplains conduct worship services in diverse settings, from makeshift chapels to open fields, providing spiritual nourishment and fostering a sense of community among service members.

Matthew 18:20 (ESV):

20. "For where two or three are gathered in my name, there am I among them."

By creating spaces for communal worship, chaplains help service members connect with their faith and each other.

Counseling During Deployment

Chaplains offer counseling and support during deployment, helping service members cope with the stresses of military life and separation from loved ones.

Proverbs 12:25 (ESV):

25. "Anxiety in a man's heart weighs him down, but a good word makes him glad."

Chaplains provide a listening ear and compassionate support, helping service members manage their emotional well-being.

Crisis Intervention in Combat Zones

Chaplains provide crisis intervention in combat zones, offering immediate support and stabilization during traumatic events.

Psalm 46:1 (ESV):

1. "God is our refuge and strength, a very present help in trouble."

Chaplains act as a stabilizing presence, providing practical assistance and emotional support during critical moments.

Expository Study with Exhaustive Strong's Concordance

To deepen our understanding of military chaplaincy, we turn to Strong's Exhaustive Concordance to explore key Hebrew and Greek terms.

Support

- Hebrew: "Ezrah" (עֶזְרָה, Strong's H5833): This term means help or support, underscoring the assistance chaplains provide (Psalm 46:1).

- Greek: "Boetheia" (βοήθεια, Strong's G996): This term means help or aid, highlighting the support offered by chaplains (Hebrews 4:16).

Resilience

- Greek: "Endureo" (ἐνδυναμόω, Strong's G1743): This term means to strengthen or empower, reflecting the role of chaplains in promoting resilience (Philippians 4:13).

Comprehensive Commentary

Providing Support and Encouragement

The biblical concept of support and encouragement is central to the role of military chaplains. The Hebrew term "ezrah" (Strong's H5833) and the Greek term "boetheia" (Strong's G996) both emphasize the act of providing help and support. Chaplains, by offering comprehensive support, help service members navigate the challenges of military life and maintain their well-being.

Promoting Resilience and Well-Being

Resilience and well-being are crucial for the mental health and overall well-being of service members. The Greek term "endureo" (Strong's G1743) highlights the importance of strengthening and empowering individuals. Chaplains, by promoting resilience, help service members develop coping strategies and maintain their mental health.

Military chaplaincy involves providing spiritual and emotional support to service members and their families, addressing the unique challenges of military life, and promoting resilience and well-being. By offering spiritual support, counseling, conducting religious services, and providing crisis intervention, chaplains play a vital role in the lives of service members. Through an exploration of biblical foundations, theological implications, and practical applications, we have gained a deeper understanding of the roles and responsibilities of military chaplains. As we continue to delve into chaplaincy in different contexts, the commitment to providing comprehensive support and promoting resilience will remain central, guiding and informing the practice of military chaplaincy.

Hospital Chaplaincy

Hospital chaplaincy involves providing spiritual care to patients, families, and healthcare staff, offering comfort, hope, and support in times of illness and crisis. Hospital chaplains play a crucial role in the healthcare setting, addressing the spiritual and emotional needs of individuals and helping them navigate the complexities of medical care and personal suffering. This chapter explores the roles and responsibilities of hospital chaplains, the unique challenges they face, and the impact of their work on patients, families, and healthcare staff.

Roles and Responsibilities of Hospital Chaplains

Hospital chaplains fulfill a range of roles and responsibilities, providing comprehensive spiritual care and support to those they serve.

Providing Spiritual Support

Hospital chaplains offer spiritual support to patients and their families, helping them find comfort and meaning in the midst of illness.

Psalm 23:4 (ESV):

4. "Even though I walk through the valley of the shadow of death, I will fear no evil, for you are with me; your rod and your staff, they comfort me."

Chaplains provide a comforting presence, helping individuals draw strength from their faith during difficult times.

Offering Emotional Support

Chaplains offer emotional support to patients and families, addressing their fears, anxieties, and emotional distress.

Psalm 34:18 (ESV):

18. "The Lord is near to the brokenhearted and saves the crushed in spirit."

By offering a listening ear and compassionate support, chaplains help alleviate emotional burdens and provide a sense of hope.

Conducting Religious Services

Chaplains conduct religious services, including prayers, sacraments, and ceremonies, providing spiritual nourishment and opportunities for communal worship.

James 5:14-15 (ESV):

14. "Is anyone among you sick? Let him call for the elders of the church, and let them pray over him, anointing him with oil in the name of the Lord."

15. "And the prayer of faith will save the one who is sick, and the Lord will raise him up. And if he has committed sins, he will be forgiven."

By facilitating religious services, chaplains provide spiritual comfort and foster a sense of community.

Crisis Intervention

Chaplains provide crisis intervention, offering immediate support during medical emergencies and critical moments.

Psalm 46:1 (ESV):

1. "God is our refuge and strength, a very present help in trouble."

Chaplains act as a stabilizing presence, providing practical assistance and emotional support during times of crisis.

Supporting Healthcare Staff

Chaplains support healthcare staff by addressing their spiritual and emotional needs, offering a listening ear, and providing resources for self-care and resilience.

Galatians 6:2 (ESV):

2. "Bear one another's burdens, and so fulfill the law of Christ."

By supporting healthcare staff, chaplains help foster a compassionate and resilient healthcare environment.

Unique Challenges of Hospital Chaplaincy

Hospital chaplains face unique challenges as they serve in a fast-paced and emotionally charged environment.

Addressing Diverse Spiritual Needs

Hospital chaplains must be prepared to address the diverse spiritual needs of patients from various religious and cultural backgrounds.

1 Corinthians 9:22 (ESV):

22. "To the weak I became weak, that I might win the weak. I have become all things to all people, that by all means I might save some."

Chaplains demonstrate cultural competence and sensitivity, providing respectful and inclusive spiritual care.

Navigating Ethical Dilemmas

Chaplains often encounter ethical dilemmas related to medical treatment, end-of-life care, and patient autonomy.

Micah 6:8 (ESV):

8. "He has told you, O man, what is good; and what does the Lord require of you but to do justice, and to love kindness, and to walk humbly with your God?"

Chaplains provide ethical guidance and support, helping patients and families navigate complex moral decisions with integrity.

Managing Personal Stress and Burnout

The emotionally demanding nature of hospital chaplaincy can lead to personal stress and burnout.

Matthew 11:28 (ESV):

28. "Come to me, all who labor and are heavy laden, and I will give you rest."

Chaplains practice self-care and seek support to maintain their own well-being and resilience.

Impact of Hospital Chaplaincy on Patients, Families, and Healthcare Staff

Hospital chaplaincy has a profound impact on the well-being and resilience of patients, families, and healthcare staff.

Providing Comfort and Hope

Chaplains provide comfort and hope to patients and families, helping them find meaning and strength in the midst of illness.

2 Corinthians 1:3-4 (ESV):

3. "Blessed be the God and Father of our Lord Jesus Christ, the Father of mercies and God of all comfort,"

4. "who comforts us in all our affliction, so that we may be able to comfort those who are in any affliction, with the comfort with which we ourselves are comforted by God."

By offering compassionate care, chaplains help individuals experience God's comfort and presence.

Enhancing Emotional Well-Being

Chaplains enhance the emotional well-being of patients and families by providing a supportive and empathetic presence.

Proverbs 12:25 (ESV):

25. "Anxiety in a man's heart weighs him down, but a good word makes him glad."

Chaplains alleviate emotional distress and provide a sense of hope and encouragement.

Supporting Healthcare Staff

Chaplains support healthcare staff by addressing their spiritual and emotional needs, helping them manage stress and maintain their well-being.

Isaiah 40:31 (ESV):

31. "But they who wait for the Lord shall renew their strength; they shall mount up with wings like eagles; they shall run and not be weary; they shall walk and not faint."

By providing support and resources, chaplains help healthcare staff sustain their compassionate care for patients.

Practical Examples of Hospital Chaplaincy

Bedside Visits

Chaplains conduct bedside visits to offer spiritual and emotional support to patients and families, providing prayers, listening, and companionship.

James 5:14-15 (ESV):

14. "Is anyone among you sick? Let him call for the elders of the church, and let them pray over him, anointing him with oil in the name of the Lord."

15. "And the prayer of faith will save the one who is sick, and the Lord will raise him up. And if he has committed sins, he will be forgiven."

By offering bedside visits, chaplains provide comfort and spiritual nourishment.

Conducting Religious Services

Chaplains conduct religious services, such as prayer meetings, communion services, and memorial services, providing opportunities for communal worship and spiritual expression.

Matthew 18:20 (ESV):

20. "For where two or three are gathered in my name, there am I among them."

By facilitating religious services, chaplains foster a sense of community and spiritual connection.

Crisis Intervention

Chaplains provide crisis intervention during medical emergencies, offering immediate support and stabilization.

Psalm 46:1 (ESV):

1. "God is our refuge and strength, a very present help in trouble."

Chaplains act as a stabilizing presence, providing practical assistance and emotional support during critical moments.

Supporting Healthcare Staff

Chaplains offer support to healthcare staff through counseling, debriefing sessions, and providing resources for self-care and resilience.

Galatians 6:2 (ESV):

2. "Bear one another's burdens, and so fulfill the law of Christ."

By supporting healthcare staff, chaplains help create a compassionate and resilient healthcare environment.

Expository Study with Exhaustive Strong's Concordance

To deepen our understanding of hospital chaplaincy, we turn to Strong's Exhaustive Concordance to explore key Hebrew and Greek terms.

Comfort

- Greek: "Paraklesis" (παράκλησις, Strong's G3874): This term means comfort or encouragement, emphasizing the act of providing support (2 Corinthians 1:3-4).

- Hebrew: "Nacham" (נָחַם, Strong's H5162): This term means to comfort or console, highlighting the role of chaplains in offering solace (Isaiah 40:1).

Support

- Hebrew: "Ezrah" (עֶזְרָה, Strong's H5833): This term means help or support, underscoring the assistance chaplains provide (Psalm 46:1).

- Greek: "Boetheia" (βοήθεια, Strong's G996): This term means help or aid, highlighting the support offered by chaplains (Hebrews 4:16).

Comprehensive Commentary

Providing Comfort and Encouragement

The biblical concept of comfort and encouragement is central to the role of hospital chaplains. The Greek term "paraklesis" (Strong's G3874) and the Hebrew term "nacham" (Strong's H5162) both emphasize the act of providing solace and support. Chaplains, by offering comfort, help individuals find hope and strength in the midst of illness and crisis.

Offering Practical Support

Support is essential for helping individuals navigate the complexities of illness and medical care. The Hebrew term "ezrah" (Strong's H5833) and the Greek term "boetheia" (Strong's G996) both highlight the importance of providing help and aid. Chaplains, by offering practical support, help individuals manage their challenges and find resilience.

Hospital chaplaincy involves providing spiritual care to patients, families, and healthcare staff, offering comfort, hope, and support in times of illness and crisis. By providing spiritual and emotional support, conducting religious services, and offering crisis intervention, chaplains play a vital role in the healthcare setting. Through an exploration of biblical foundations, theological implications, and practical applications, we have gained a deeper understanding of the roles and responsibilities of hospital chaplains. As we continue to delve into chaplaincy in different contexts, the commitment to providing comprehensive support and promoting well-being will remain central, guiding and informing the practice of hospital chaplaincy.

Prison Chaplaincy

Prison chaplaincy involves serving incarcerated individuals by offering spiritual guidance, support, and opportunities for personal growth and transformation. Prison chaplains play a vital role in addressing the spiritual, emotional, and moral needs of inmates, providing a source of hope and rehabilitation in a challenging environment. This chapter explores the roles and responsibilities of prison chaplains, the unique challenges they face, and the impact of their work on inmates and the broader correctional community.

Roles and Responsibilities of Prison Chaplains

Prison chaplains fulfill a range of roles and responsibilities, providing comprehensive spiritual care and support to those they serve.

Providing Spiritual Guidance

Prison chaplains offer spiritual guidance to inmates, helping them explore their faith and find meaning and purpose in their lives.

Matthew 25:36 (ESV):

36. "I was naked and you clothed me, I was sick and you visited me, I was in prison and you came to me."

Chaplains provide a spiritual presence, helping inmates connect with their faith and find hope and redemption.

Offering Emotional Support

Chaplains offer emotional support to inmates, addressing their fears, anxieties, and emotional distress.

Psalm 34:18 (ESV):

18. "The Lord is near to the brokenhearted and saves the crushed in spirit."

By offering a listening ear and compassionate support, chaplains help alleviate emotional burdens and provide a sense of hope.

Conducting Religious Services

Chaplains conduct religious services, including prayers, sacraments, and ceremonies, providing spiritual nourishment and opportunities for communal worship.

Hebrews 10:24-25 (ESV):

24. "And let us consider how to stir up one another to love and good works,"

25. "not neglecting to meet together, as is the habit of some, but encouraging one another, and all the more as you see the Day drawing near."

By facilitating religious services, chaplains provide spiritual comfort and foster a sense of community among inmates.

Supporting Rehabilitation and Personal Growth

Chaplains support the rehabilitation and personal growth of inmates by offering programs and resources that promote moral and spiritual development.

Romans 12:2 (ESV):

2. "Do not be conformed to this world, but be transformed by the renewal of your mind, that by testing you may discern what is the will of God, what is good and acceptable and perfect."

Chaplains provide opportunities for inmates to engage in personal reflection and transformation, helping them develop positive attitudes and behaviors.

Crisis Intervention

Chaplains provide crisis intervention, offering immediate support during times of personal or institutional crisis.

Psalm 46:1 (ESV):

1. "God is our refuge and strength, a very present help in trouble."

Chaplains act as a stabilizing presence, providing practical assistance and emotional support during critical moments.

Unique Challenges of Prison Chaplaincy

Prison chaplains face unique challenges as they serve in a highly controlled and often volatile environment.

Navigating the Correctional Environment

Chaplains must navigate the complexities of the correctional environment, balancing security concerns with their pastoral responsibilities.

Matthew 10:16 (ESV):

16. "Behold, I am sending you out as sheep in the midst of wolves, so be wise as serpents and innocent as doves."

Chaplains exercise wisdom and prudence, building trust with both inmates and correctional staff while maintaining their pastoral integrity.

Addressing Diverse Spiritual Needs

Prison chaplains must be prepared to address the diverse spiritual needs of inmates from various religious and cultural backgrounds.

1 Corinthians 9:22 (ESV):

22. "To the weak I became weak, that I might win the weak. I have become all things to all people, that by all means I might save some."

Chaplains demonstrate cultural competence and sensitivity, providing respectful and inclusive spiritual care.

Managing Personal Stress and Burnout

The emotionally demanding nature of prison chaplaincy can lead to personal stress and burnout.

Matthew 11:28 (ESV):

28. "Come to me, all who labor and are heavy laden, and I will give you rest."

Chaplains practice self-care and seek support to maintain their own well-being and resilience.

Impact of Prison Chaplaincy on Inmates and the Correctional Community

Prison chaplaincy has a profound impact on the well-being and rehabilitation of inmates, as well as on the broader correctional community.

Promoting Personal Transformation

Chaplains promote personal transformation by providing spiritual guidance and support, helping inmates develop positive attitudes and behaviors.

2 Corinthians 5:17 (ESV):

17. "Therefore, if anyone is in Christ, he is a new creation. The old has passed away; behold, the new has come."

By offering opportunities for spiritual growth, chaplains help inmates experience personal transformation and renewal.

Enhancing Emotional Well-Being

Chaplains enhance the emotional well-being of inmates by providing a supportive and empathetic presence.

Proverbs 12:25 (ESV):

25. "Anxiety in a man's heart weighs him down, but a good word makes him glad."

Chaplains alleviate emotional distress and provide a sense of hope and encouragement.

Fostering a Sense of Community

Chaplains foster a sense of community among inmates by facilitating religious services and communal activities.

Hebrews 10:24-25 (ESV):

24. "And let us consider how to stir up one another to love and good works,"

25. "not neglecting to meet together, as is the habit of some, but encouraging one another, and all the more as you see the Day drawing near."

By creating opportunities for communal worship and support, chaplains help inmates build supportive relationships and a sense of belonging.

Practical Examples of Prison Chaplaincy

Conducting Worship Services

Chaplains conduct worship services within the correctional facility, providing spiritual nourishment and fostering a sense of community among inmates.

Matthew 18:20 (ESV):

20. "For where two or three are gathered in my name, there am I among them."

By facilitating worship services, chaplains help inmates connect with their faith and each other.

Offering Counseling and Support

Chaplains offer counseling and support to inmates, helping them navigate the challenges of incarceration and personal issues.

Proverbs 12:25 (ESV):

25. "Anxiety in a man's heart weighs him down, but a good word makes him glad."

Chaplains provide a listening ear and compassionate support, helping inmates manage their emotional well-being.

Supporting Rehabilitation Programs

Chaplains support rehabilitation programs that promote personal growth and transformation, offering classes, workshops, and one-on-one mentoring.

Romans 12:2 (ESV):

2. "Do not be conformed to this world, but be transformed by the renewal of your mind, that by testing you may discern what is the will of God, what is good and acceptable and perfect."

Chaplains provide opportunities for inmates to engage in personal reflection and development, supporting their rehabilitation and reintegration.

Providing Crisis Intervention

Chaplains provide crisis intervention during personal or institutional crises, offering immediate support and stabilization.

Psalm 46:1 (ESV):

1. "God is our refuge and strength, a very present help in trouble."

Chaplains act as a stabilizing presence, providing practical assistance and emotional support during critical moments.

Expository Study with Exhaustive Strong's Concordance

To deepen our understanding of prison chaplaincy, we turn to Strong's Exhaustive Concordance to explore key Hebrew and Greek terms.

Support

- Hebrew: "Ezrah" (עֶזְרָה, Strong's H5833): This term means help or support, underscoring the assistance chaplains provide (Psalm 46:1).

- Greek: "Boetheia" (βοήθεια, Strong's G996): This term means help or aid, highlighting the support offered by chaplains (Hebrews 4:16).

Transformation

- Greek: "Metamorphoo" (μεταμορφόω, Strong's G3339): This term means to transform or change, reflecting the role of chaplains in promoting personal transformation (Romans 12:2).

Comprehensive Commentary

Providing Support and Encouragement

The biblical concept of support and encouragement is central to the role of prison chaplains. The Hebrew term "ezrah" (Strong's H5833) and the Greek term "boetheia" (Strong's G996) both emphasize the act of providing help and support. Chaplains, by offering comprehensive support, help inmates navigate the challenges of incarceration and find hope and resilience.

Promoting Personal Transformation

Transformation is a key goal of prison chaplaincy, helping inmates develop positive attitudes and behaviors. The Greek term "metamorphoo" (Strong's G3339) highlights the importance of personal change and renewal. Chaplains, by promoting transformation, help inmates experience personal growth and rehabilitation.

Prison chaplaincy involves serving incarcerated individuals by offering spiritual guidance, support, and opportunities for personal growth and transformation. By providing spiritual and emotional support, conducting religious services, supporting rehabilitation programs, and offering crisis intervention, chaplains play a vital role in the correctional environment. Through an exploration of biblical foundations, theological implications, and practical applications, we have gained a deeper understanding of the roles and responsibilities of prison chaplains. As we continue to delve into chaplaincy in different contexts, the commitment to providing comprehensive support and promoting personal transformation will remain central, guiding and informing the practice of prison chaplaincy.

University Chaplaincy

University chaplaincy involves supporting students, faculty, and staff, fostering a sense of community and addressing the spiritual and emotional needs of the academic environment. University chaplains play a crucial role in creating a supportive and inclusive campus culture, offering guidance, counseling, and opportunities for spiritual growth and development. This chapter explores the roles and responsibilities of university chaplains, the unique challenges they face, and the impact of their work on the academic community.

Roles and Responsibilities of University Chaplains

University chaplains fulfill a range of roles and responsibilities, providing comprehensive spiritual care and support to the campus community.

Providing Spiritual Guidance

University chaplains offer spiritual guidance to students, faculty, and staff, helping them explore their faith and find meaning and purpose in their academic and personal lives.

Proverbs 3:5-6 (ESV):

5. "Trust in the Lord with all your heart, and do not lean on your own understanding."

6. "In all your ways acknowledge him, and he will make straight your paths."

Chaplains provide spiritual direction, helping individuals connect with their faith and navigate the complexities of university life.

Offering Emotional Support

Chaplains offer emotional support to students, faculty, and staff, addressing their fears, anxieties, and emotional distress.

Psalm 34:18 (ESV):

18. "The Lord is near to the brokenhearted and saves the crushed in spirit."

By offering a listening ear and compassionate support, chaplains help alleviate emotional burdens and provide a sense of hope and encouragement.

Conducting Religious Services

Chaplains conduct religious services, including prayers, sacraments, and ceremonies, providing spiritual nourishment and opportunities for communal worship.

Hebrews 10:24 25 (ESV):

24. "And let us consider how to stir up one another to love and good works,"

25. "not neglecting to meet together, as is the habit of some, but encouraging one another, and all the more as you see the Day drawing near."

By facilitating religious services, chaplains provide spiritual comfort and foster a sense of community among the academic population.

Supporting Academic and Personal Development

Chaplains support the academic and personal development of students by offering programs and resources that promote moral and spiritual growth.

James 1:5 (ESV):

5. "If any of you lacks wisdom, let him ask God, who gives generously to all without reproach, and it will be given him."

Chaplains provide opportunities for students to engage in personal reflection and development, helping them grow academically and spiritually.

Crisis Intervention

Chaplains provide crisis intervention, offering immediate support during times of personal or institutional crisis.

Psalm 46:1 (ESV):

1. "God is our refuge and strength, a very present help in trouble."

Chaplains act as a stabilizing presence, providing practical assistance and emotional support during critical moments.

Unique Challenges of University Chaplaincy

University chaplains face unique challenges as they serve in a diverse and dynamic academic environment.

Addressing Diverse Spiritual Needs

University chaplains must be prepared to address the diverse spiritual needs of students, faculty, and staff from various religious and cultural backgrounds.

1 Corinthians 9:22 (ESV):

22. "To the weak I became weak, that I might win the weak. I have become all things to all people, that by all means I might save some."

Chaplains demonstrate cultural competence and sensitivity, providing respectful and inclusive spiritual care.

Navigating Academic Pressures

Chaplains help students navigate the pressures and stresses associated with academic life, including exams, deadlines, and academic performance.

Philippians 4:6-7 (ESV):

6. "Do not be anxious about anything, but in everything by prayer and supplication with thanksgiving let your requests be made known to God."

7. "And the peace of God, which surpasses all understanding, will guard your hearts and your minds in Christ Jesus."

Chaplains offer support and encouragement, helping students manage stress and maintain their well-being.

Managing Personal Stress and Burnout

The emotionally demanding nature of university chaplaincy can lead to personal stress and burnout.

Matthew 11:28 (ESV):

28. "Come to me, all who labor and are heavy laden, and I will give you rest."

Chaplains practice self-care and seek support to maintain their own well-being and resilience.

Impact of University Chaplaincy on the Academic Community

University chaplaincy has a profound impact on the well-being and development of students, faculty, and staff, as well as on the broader academic community.

Promoting Personal and Spiritual Growth

Chaplains promote personal and spiritual growth by providing guidance and support, helping individuals develop positive attitudes and behaviors.

2 Peter 3:18 (ESV):

18. "But grow in the grace and knowledge of our Lord and Savior Jesus Christ. To him be the glory both now and to the day of eternity. Amen."

By offering opportunities for spiritual exploration and development, chaplains help individuals grow in their faith and personal lives.

Enhancing Emotional Well-Being

Chaplains enhance the emotional well-being of students, faculty, and staff by providing a supportive and empathetic presence.

Proverbs 12:25 (ESV):

25. "Anxiety in a man's heart weighs him down, but a good word makes him glad."

Chaplains alleviate emotional distress and provide a sense of hope and encouragement.

Fostering a Sense of Community

Chaplains foster a sense of community on campus by facilitating religious services, communal activities, and support groups.

Hebrews 10:24-25 (ESV):

24. "And let us consider how to stir up one another to love and good works,"

25. "not neglecting to meet together, as is the habit of some, but encouraging one another, and all the more as you see the Day drawing near."

By creating opportunities for communal worship and support, chaplains help build supportive relationships and a sense of belonging within the academic community.

Practical Examples of University Chaplaincy

Conducting Worship Services

Chaplains conduct worship services on campus, providing spiritual nourishment and fostering a sense of community among students, faculty, and staff.

Matthew 18:20 (ESV):

20. "For where two or three are gathered in my name, there am I among them."

By facilitating worship services, chaplains help individuals connect with their faith and each other.

Offering Counseling and Support

Chaplains offer counseling and support to students, faculty, and staff, helping them navigate the challenges of academic and personal life.

Proverbs 12:25 (ESV):

25. "Anxiety in a man's heart weighs him down, but a good word makes him glad."

Chaplains provide a listening ear and compassionate support, helping individuals manage their emotional well-being.

Supporting Academic and Personal Development

Chaplains support academic and personal development through programs, workshops, and one-on-one mentoring that promote moral and spiritual growth.

James 1:5 (ESV):

5. "If any of you lacks wisdom, let him ask God, who gives generously to all without reproach, and it will be given him."

Chaplains provide opportunities for individuals to engage in personal reflection and development, supporting their academic and spiritual growth.

Providing Crisis Intervention

Chaplains provide crisis intervention during personal or institutional crises, offering immediate support and stabilization.

Psalm 46:1 (ESV):

1. "God is our refuge and strength, a very present help in trouble."

Chaplains act as a stabilizing presence, providing practical assistance and emotional support during critical moments.

Expository Study with Exhaustive Strong's Concordance

To deepen our understanding of university chaplaincy, we turn to Strong's Exhaustive Concordance to explore key Hebrew and Greek terms.

Guidance

- Hebrew: "Yaats" (יָעַץ, Strong's H3289): This term means to advise or counsel, reflecting the guidance chaplains provide (Proverbs 3:5-6).

- Greek: "Hodegeo" (ὁδηγέω, Strong's G3594): This term means to guide, emphasizing the role of chaplains in providing direction (John 16:13).

Support

- Hebrew: "Ezrah" (עֶזְרָה, Strong's H5833): This term means help or support, underscoring the assistance chaplains provide (Psalm 46:1).

- Greek: "Boetheia" (βοήθεια, Strong's G996): This term means help or aid, highlighting the support offered by chaplains (Hebrews 4:16).

Comprehensive Commentary

Providing Guidance and Support

The biblical concept of guidance and support is central to the role of university chaplains. The Hebrew term "yaats" (Strong's H3289) and the Greek term "hodegeo" (Strong's G3594) both emphasize the importance of providing direction and counsel. Chaplains, by offering guidance and support, help individuals navigate the complexities of academic and personal life.

Promoting Personal and Spiritual Growth

Growth is a key goal of university chaplaincy, helping individuals develop positive attitudes and behaviors. The Greek term "auxano" (αὐξάνω, Strong's G837) highlights the importance of growth and development. Chaplains, by promoting personal and spiritual growth, help individuals experience transformation and renewal.

University chaplaincy involves supporting students, faculty, and staff, fostering a sense of community and addressing the spiritual and emotional needs of the academic environment. By providing spiritual and emotional support, conducting religious services, supporting academic and personal development, and offering crisis intervention, chaplains play a vital role in the academic community. Through an exploration of biblical foundations, theological implications, and practical applications, we have gained a deeper understanding of the roles and responsibilities of university chaplains. As we continue to delve into chaplaincy in different contexts, the commitment to providing comprehensive support and promoting personal and spiritual growth will remain central, guiding and informing the practice of university chaplaincy.

Workplace Chaplaincy

Workplace chaplaincy involves providing spiritual care and support in corporate settings, promoting employee well-being, and addressing issues related to work-life balance, stress, and ethical challenges. Workplace chaplains play a crucial role in fostering a positive work environment, offering guidance, counseling, and support to employees. This chapter explores the roles and responsibilities of workplace chaplains, the unique challenges they face, and the impact of their work on employees and the corporate culture.

Roles and Responsibilities of Workplace Chaplains

Workplace chaplains fulfill a range of roles and responsibilities, providing comprehensive spiritual care and support to employees.

Providing Spiritual Guidance

Workplace chaplains offer spiritual guidance to employees, helping them explore their faith and find meaning and purpose in their work and personal lives.

Proverbs 16:3 (ESV):

3. "Commit your work to the Lord, and your plans will be established."

Chaplains provide spiritual direction, helping employees integrate their faith with their work and navigate the complexities of the corporate environment.

Offering Emotional Support

Chaplains offer emotional support to employees, addressing their fears, anxieties, and emotional distress.

Psalm 34:18 (ESV):

18. "The Lord is near to the brokenhearted and saves the crushed in spirit."

By offering a listening ear and compassionate support, chaplains help alleviate emotional burdens and provide a sense of hope and encouragement.

Promoting Work-Life Balance

Chaplains help employees achieve a healthy work-life balance, addressing issues related to stress, burnout, and time management.

Matthew 11:28-30 (ESV):

28. "Come to me, all who labor and are heavy laden, and I will give you rest."

29. "Take my yoke upon you, and learn from me, for I am gentle and lowly in heart, and you will find rest for your souls."

30. "For my yoke is easy, and my burden is light."

Chaplains provide guidance and support, helping employees find rest and balance in their lives.

Addressing Ethical Challenges

Chaplains offer guidance and support in addressing ethical challenges in the workplace, helping employees navigate complex moral and ethical decisions.

Micah 6:8 (ESV):

8. "He has told you, O man, what is good; and what does the Lord require of you but to do justice, and to love kindness, and to walk humbly with your God?"

Chaplains provide ethical guidance, helping employees act with integrity and uphold ethical standards in their work.

Conducting Religious Services

Chaplains conduct religious services, including prayers, sacraments, and ceremonies, providing spiritual nourishment and opportunities for communal worship.

Matthew 18:20 (ESV):

20. "For where two or three are gathered in my name, there am I among them."

By facilitating religious services, chaplains foster a sense of community and spiritual connection among employees.

Unique Challenges of Workplace Chaplaincy

Workplace chaplains face unique challenges as they serve in a diverse and dynamic corporate environment.

Addressing Diverse Spiritual Needs

Workplace chaplains must be prepared to address the diverse spiritual needs of employees from various religious and cultural backgrounds.

1 Corinthians 9:22 (ESV):

22. "To the weak I became weak, that I might win the weak. I have become all things to all people, that by all means I might save some."

Chaplains demonstrate cultural competence and sensitivity, providing respectful and inclusive spiritual care.

Navigating Corporate Culture

Chaplains must navigate the complexities of corporate culture, balancing their pastoral responsibilities with the demands of the business environment.

Matthew 10:16 (ESV):

16. "Behold, I am sending you out as sheep in the midst of wolves, so be wise as serpents and innocent as doves."

Chaplains exercise wisdom and prudence, building trust with employees and management while maintaining their pastoral integrity.

Managing Personal Stress and Burnout

The emotionally demanding nature of workplace chaplaincy can lead to personal stress and burnout.

Matthew 11:28 (ESV):

28. "Come to me, all who labor and are heavy laden, and I will give you rest."

Chaplains practice self-care and seek support to maintain their own well-being and resilience.

Impact of Workplace Chaplaincy on Employees and Corporate Culture

Workplace chaplaincy has a profound impact on the well-being and resilience of employees, as well as on the overall corporate culture.

Promoting Employee Well-Being

Chaplains promote employee well-being by providing spiritual and emotional support, helping employees manage stress and maintain their mental health.

Philippians 4:6-7 (ESV):

6. "Do not be anxious about anything, but in everything by prayer and supplication with thanksgiving let your requests be made known to God."

7. "And the peace of God, which surpasses all understanding, will guard your hearts and your minds in Christ Jesus."

By fostering a sense of spiritual peace and resilience, chaplains help employees navigate the challenges of the workplace.

Enhancing Ethical Standards

Chaplains enhance ethical standards in the workplace by providing guidance and support in addressing ethical challenges.

Proverbs 11:3 (ESV):

3. "The integrity of the upright guides them, but the crookedness of the treacherous destroys them."

By promoting ethical behavior and integrity, chaplains help create a culture of trust and respect within the organization.

Fostering a Sense of Community

Chaplains foster a sense of community in the workplace by facilitating communal activities, religious services, and support groups.

Hebrews 10:24-25 (ESV):

24. "And let us consider how to stir up one another to love and good works,"

25. "not neglecting to meet together, as is the habit of some, but encouraging one another, and all the more as you see the Day drawing near."

By creating opportunities for communal support and connection, chaplains help employees build supportive relationships and a sense of belonging.

Practical Examples of Workplace Chaplaincy

Offering Counseling and Support

Chaplains offer counseling and support to employees, helping them navigate personal and work-related challenges.

Proverbs 12:25 (ESV):

25. "Anxiety in a man's heart weighs him down, but a good word makes him glad."

Chaplains provide a listening ear and compassionate support, helping employees manage their emotional well-being.

Conducting Religious Services

Chaplains conduct religious services within the workplace, providing spiritual nourishment and fostering a sense of community among employees.

Matthew 18:20 (ESV):

20. "For where two or three are gathered in my name, there am I among them."

By facilitating religious services, chaplains help employees connect with their faith and each other.

Providing Crisis Intervention

Chaplains provide crisis intervention during personal or workplace crises, offering immediate support and stabilization.

Psalm 46:1 (ESV):

1. "God is our refuge and strength, a very present help in trouble."

Chaplains act as a stabilizing presence, providing practical assistance and emotional support during critical moments.

Expository Study with Exhaustive Strong's Concordance

To deepen our understanding of workplace chaplaincy, we turn to Strong's Exhaustive Concordance to explore key Hebrew and Greek terms.

Guidance

- Hebrew: "Yaats" (יָעַץ, Strong's H3289): This term means to advise or counsel, reflecting the guidance chaplains provide (Proverbs 16:3).

- Greek: "Hodegeo" (ὁδηγέω, Strong's G3594): This term means to guide, emphasizing the role of chaplains in providing direction (John 16:13).

Support

- Hebrew: "Ezrah" (עֶזְרָה, Strong's H5833): This term means help or support, underscoring the assistance chaplains provide (Psalm 46:1).

- Greek: "Boetheia" (βοήθεια, Strong's G996): This term means help or aid, highlighting the support offered by chaplains (Hebrews 4:16).

Comprehensive Commentary
Providing Guidance and Support

The biblical concept of guidance and support is central to the role of workplace chaplains. The Hebrew term "yaats" (Strong's H3289) and the Greek term "hodegeo" (Strong's G3594) both emphasize the importance of providing direction and counsel. Chaplains, by offering guidance and support, help employees navigate the complexities of work and personal life.

Promoting Ethical Behavior

Ethical behavior is a key goal of workplace chaplaincy, helping employees act with integrity and uphold ethical standards. The Greek term "ethos" (ἦθος, Strong's G1485) highlights the importance of moral character. Chaplains, by promoting ethical behavior, help create a culture of trust and respect within the organization.

Workplace chaplaincy involves providing spiritual care and support in corporate settings, promoting employee well-being, and addressing issues related to work-life balance, stress, and ethical challenges. By providing spiritual and emotional support, promoting ethical behavior, and offering crisis intervention, chaplains play a vital role in the corporate environment. Through an exploration of biblical foundations, theological implications, and practical applications, we have gained a deeper understanding of the roles and responsibilities of workplace chaplains. As we continue to delve into chaplaincy in different contexts, the commitment to providing comprehensive support and promoting employee well-being will remain central, guiding and informing the practice of workplace chaplaincy.

CHAPTER 06

PASTORAL CARE AND COUNSELING

The Nature of Pastoral Care

Pastoral care involves providing holistic support, addressing the spiritual, emotional, and relational needs of individuals. This comprehensive approach is essential for chaplains, who use various techniques such as active listening, empathy, and reflective questioning to help individuals explore their concerns and find meaning and hope. This chapter explores the nature of pastoral care, its biblical foundations, theological implications, and practical applications.

Biblical Foundations of Pastoral Care

The Bible provides a rich foundation for understanding and practicing pastoral care, emphasizing the importance of compassion, empathy, and holistic support.

Compassion and Care

Compassion is a fundamental aspect of pastoral care, reflecting God's compassionate nature.

Psalm 103:13-14 (ESV):

13. "As a father shows compassion to his children, so the Lord shows compassion to those who fear him."

14. "For he knows our frame; he remembers that we are dust."

The Hebrew word for "compassion" (רָחַם, racham, Strong's H7355) conveys a deep, parental love and care. Chaplains, by offering compassion, reflect this divine attribute and provide comfort and support.

Bearing One Another's Burdens

Pastoral care involves bearing one another's burdens, and demonstrating love and solidarity.

Galatians 6:2 (ESV):

2. "Bear one another's burdens, and so fulfill the law of Christ."

The Greek word for "burdens" (βάρος, baros, Strong's G922) refers to heavy loads or difficulties. By helping individuals carry their burdens, chaplains fulfill the law of Christ, which is grounded in love and compassion.

Providing Comfort

Providing comfort is a central aspect of pastoral care, offering solace and encouragement to those in distress.

2 Corinthians 1:3-4 (ESV):

3. "Blessed be the God and Father of our Lord Jesus Christ, the Father of mercies and God of all comfort,"

4. "who comforts us in all our affliction, so that we may be able to comfort those who are in any affliction, with the comfort with which we ourselves are comforted by God."

The Greek word for "comfort" (παράκλησις, paraklesis, Strong's G3874) emphasizes the act of coming alongside someone to provide encouragement and support.

Theological Implications of Pastoral Care

Pastoral care has profound theological implications, reflecting key aspects of God's relationship with humanity and His expectations for His people.

Reflecting God's Compassion

Pastoral care reflects God's compassion and concern for His people.

Psalm 34:18 (ESV):

18. "The Lord is near to the brokenhearted and saves the crushed in spirit."

The Hebrew word for "saves" (יָשַׁע, yasha, Strong's H3467) signifies deliverance and rescue. Chaplains, by offering support, reflect God's desire to heal and restore the brokenhearted.

Participating in God's Healing Work

Pastoral care is a means of participating in God's healing work, addressing the holistic needs of individuals.

Psalm 147:3 (ESV):

3. "He heals the brokenhearted and binds up their wounds."

The Hebrew word for "heals" (רָפָא, rapha, Strong's H7495) signifies restoration and wholeness. Chaplains, through their ministry, contribute to this healing process, offering support that addresses emotional, spiritual, and physical wounds.

Practical Applications of Pastoral Care

Chaplains provide pastoral care through various practical applications, addressing the diverse needs of those they serve.

Active Listening

Active listening involves fully engaging with the individual, showing empathy, and providing a safe space for them to express their thoughts and feelings.

James 1:19 (ESV):

19. "Know this, my beloved brothers: let every person be quick to hear, slow to speak, slow to anger."

By practicing active listening, chaplains show empathy and understanding, helping individuals feel heard and valued.

Offering Empathy

Empathy is the ability to understand and share the feelings of others, demonstrating compassion and support.

Romans 12:15 (ESV):

15. "Rejoice with those who rejoice, weep with those who weep."

The Greek word for "weep" (κλαίω, klaio, Strong's G2799) highlights the act of sharing in the emotional experiences of others. Chaplains who demonstrate empathy are able to provide compassionate care and support.

Reflective Questioning

Reflective questioning involves asking thoughtful questions that help individuals explore their concerns and find meaning and hope.

Proverbs 20:5 (ESV):

5. "The purpose in a man's heart is like deep water, but a man of understanding will draw it out."

By using reflective questioning, chaplains help individuals gain insights into their experiences and discover new perspectives.

Expository Study with Exhaustive Strong's Concordance

To deepen our understanding of pastoral care, we turn to Strong's Exhaustive Concordance to explore key Hebrew and Greek terms.

Compassion

- Hebrew: "Racham" (רָחַם, Strong's H7355): This term means compassion or mercy, reflecting the compassionate care chaplains provide (Psalm 103:13-14).

- Greek: "Splagchnizomai" (σπλαγχνίζομαι, Strong's G4697): This term means to be moved with compassion, highlighting the deep emotional response that motivates action (Matthew 9:36).

Comfort

- Greek: "Paraklesis" (παράκλησις, Strong's G3874): This term means comfort or encouragement, emphasizing the act of providing support (2 Corinthians 1:3-4).

- Hebrew: "Nacham" (נָחַם, Strong's H5162): This term means to comfort or console, highlighting the role of chaplains in offering solace (Isaiah 40:1).

Comprehensive Commentary

Compassion and Empathy in Pastoral Care

The biblical concept of compassion and empathy is central to the nature of pastoral care. The Hebrew term "racham" (Strong's H7355) and the Greek term "splagchnizomai" (Strong's G4697) both emphasize the deep emotional response that motivates compassionate action. Chaplains, by demonstrating compassion and empathy, provide support that reflects the heart of God.

Providing Comfort and Encouragement

Comfort and encouragement are essential components of pastoral care. The Greek term "paraklesis" (Strong's G3874) and the Hebrew term "nacham" (Strong's H5162) both emphasize the act of providing solace and support. Chaplains, by offering comfort, help individuals find hope and strength in the midst of their struggles.

Practical Examples of Pastoral Care

Active Listening and Empathy

Chaplains practice active listening and empathy by fully engaging with individuals, providing a safe space for them to express their thoughts and feelings.

James 1:19 (ESV):

19. "Know this, my beloved brothers: let every person be quick to hear, slow to speak, slow to anger."

By showing empathy and understanding, chaplains help individuals feel heard and valued.

Reflective Questioning and Guidance

Chaplains use reflective questioning to help individuals explore their concerns and gain new insights.

Proverbs 20:5 (ESV):

5. "The purpose in a man's heart is like deep water, but a man of understanding will draw it out."

By asking thoughtful questions, chaplains help individuals discover new perspectives and find meaning and hope.

Providing Comfort and Encouragement

Chaplains provide comfort and encouragement to those in distress, offering solace and support.

2 Corinthians 1:3-4 (ESV):

3. "Blessed be the God and Father of our Lord Jesus Christ, the Father of mercies and God of all comfort,"

4. "who comforts us in all our affliction, so that we may be able to comfort those who are in any affliction, with the comfort with which we ourselves are comforted by God."

By offering comfort, chaplains help individuals experience God's presence and peace.

Pastoral care involves providing holistic support, addressing the spiritual, emotional, and relational needs of individuals. By practicing active listening, empathy, and reflective questioning, chaplains help individuals explore their concerns and find meaning and hope. Through an exploration of biblical foundations, theological implications, and practical applications, we have gained a deeper understanding of the nature of pastoral care. As we continue to delve into pastoral care and counseling, the commitment to providing compassionate support and fostering personal growth will remain central, guiding and informing the practice of chaplaincy.

Counseling Techniques

Chaplains employ a range of counseling techniques to address specific issues and promote healing and growth. These techniques include cognitive-behavioral therapy (CBT), solution-focused therapy, and narrative therapy, among others. By utilizing these approaches, chaplains can effectively support individuals in navigating their challenges and finding paths to personal growth and healing. This chapter explores the principles and applications of these counseling techniques in the context of chaplaincy.

Cognitive-behavioral therapy (CBT)

Cognitive-behavioral therapy (CBT) is a widely used counseling technique that focuses on identifying and changing negative thought patterns and behaviors.

Principles of CBT

CBT is based on the idea that our thoughts, feelings, and behaviors are interconnected. By changing negative thought patterns, individuals can improve their emotional well-being and behavior.

Romans 12:2 (ESV):

2. "Do not be conformed to this world, but be transformed by the renewal of your mind, that by testing you may discern what is the will of God, what is good and acceptable and perfect."

This verse highlights the importance of renewing the mind, which is central to the principles of CBT.

Applications of CBT in Chaplaincy

Chaplains can use CBT to help individuals identify and challenge negative thought patterns and develop healthier ways of thinking and behaving.

Philippians 4:8 (ESV):

8. "Finally, brothers, whatever is true, whatever is honorable, whatever is just, whatever is pure, whatever is lovely, whatever is commendable, if there is any excellence, if there is anything worthy of praise, think about these things."

By encouraging individuals to focus on positive and constructive thoughts, chaplains can help them experience greater emotional well-being.

Solution-Focused Therapy

Solution-focused therapy is a counseling technique that emphasizes finding solutions to problems rather than focusing on the problems themselves.

Principles of Solution-Focused Therapy

Solution-focused therapy is based on the idea that individuals have the resources and strengths to solve their own problems. The therapist's role is to help individuals identify and build on these strengths.

Proverbs 3:5-6 (ESV):

5. "Trust in the Lord with all your heart, and do not lean on your own understanding."

6. "In all your ways acknowledge him, and he will make straight your paths."

This passage emphasizes the importance of trusting in one's own abilities and seeking guidance to find solutions.

Applications of Solution-Focused Therapy in Chaplaincy

Chaplains can use solution-focused therapy to help individuals identify their strengths and resources and develop practical solutions to their challenges.

James 1:5 (ESV):

5. "If any of you lacks wisdom, let him ask God, who gives generously to all without reproach, and it will be given him."

By helping individuals seek wisdom and identify practical solutions, chaplains can support their personal growth and problem-solving abilities.

Narrative Therapy

Narrative therapy is a counseling technique that focuses on helping individuals reframe their personal stories to promote healing and growth.

Principles of Narrative Therapy

Narrative therapy is based on the idea that individuals make sense of their lives through the stories they tell about themselves. By reframing these stories, individuals can create new, empowering narratives.

2 Corinthians 5:17 (ESV):

17. "Therefore, if anyone is in Christ, he is a new creation. The old has passed away; behold, the new has come."

This verse highlights the transformative power of creating new narratives, which is central to narrative therapy.

Applications of Narrative Therapy in Chaplaincy

Chaplains can use narrative therapy to help individuals reframe their personal stories in a way that promotes healing and empowerment.

Psalm 40:1-3 (ESV):

1. "I waited patiently for the Lord; he inclined to me and heard my cry."

2. "He drew me up from the pit of destruction, out of the miry bog, and set my feet upon a rock, making my steps secure."

3. "He put a new song in my mouth, a song of praise to our God. Many will see and fear, and put their trust in the Lord."

By helping individuals create new, positive narratives about their lives, chaplains can support their journey toward healing and growth.

Expository Study with Exhaustive Strong's Concordance

To deepen our understanding of these counseling techniques, we turn to Strong's Exhaustive Concordance to explore key Hebrew and Greek terms.

Mind Renewal

- Greek: "Metamorphoo" (μεταμορφόω, Strong's G3339): This term means to transform or change, reflecting the process of renewing the mind (Romans 12:2).

Wisdom and Guidance

- Hebrew: "Chokmah" (חָכְמָה, Strong's H2451): This term means wisdom, highlighting the importance of seeking guidance and wisdom (Proverbs 3:5-6).

- Greek: "Sophia" (σοφία, Strong's G4678): This term means wisdom, emphasizing the role of wisdom in finding solutions (James 1:5).

New Creation

- Greek: "Kainos" (καινός, Strong's G2537): This term means new or fresh, underscoring the transformative power of new narratives (2 Corinthians 5:17).

Comprehensive Commentary

Renewing the Mind Through CBT

The biblical concept of renewing the mind is central to the principles of CBT. The Greek term "metamorphoo" (Strong's G3339) highlights the transformative power of changing thought patterns. Chaplains, by helping individuals identify and challenge negative thoughts, can support their journey toward emotional and spiritual renewal.

Seeking Wisdom and Solutions Through Solution-Focused Therapy

Wisdom and guidance are essential components of solution-focused therapy. The Hebrew term "chokmah" (Strong's H2451) and the Greek term "sophia" (Strong's

G4678) both emphasize the importance of seeking wisdom and finding practical solutions. Chaplains, by helping individuals identify their strengths and seek wisdom, can support their problem-solving abilities and personal growth.

Reframing Personal Narratives Through Narrative Therapy

The concept of new creation is central to narrative therapy. The Greek term "kainos" (Strong's G2537) underscores the transformative power of creating new narratives. Chaplains, by helping individuals reframe their personal stories, can support their journey toward healing and empowerment.

Practical Examples of Counseling Techniques in Chaplaincy

Using CBT to Address Negative Thought Patterns

Chaplains can use CBT to help individuals identify and challenge negative thought patterns, promoting healthier ways of thinking and behaving.

Philippians 4:8 (ESV):

8. "Finally, brothers, whatever is true, whatever is honorable, whatever is just, whatever is pure, whatever is lovely, whatever is commendable, if there is any excellence, if there is anything worthy of praise, think about these things."

By encouraging individuals to focus on positive and constructive thoughts, chaplains can help them experience greater emotional well-being.

Using Solution-Focused Therapy to Find Practical Solutions

Chaplains can use solution-focused therapy to help individuals identify their strengths and develop practical solutions to their challenges.

James 1:5 (ESV):

5. "If any of you lacks wisdom, let him ask God, who gives generously to all without reproach, and it will be given him."

By helping individuals seek wisdom and identify practical solutions, chaplains can support their personal growth and problem-solving abilities.

Using Narrative Therapy to Reframe Personal Stories

Chaplains can use narrative therapy to help individuals reframe their personal stories in a way that promotes healing and empowerment.

Psalm 40:1-3 (ESV):

1. "I waited patiently for the Lord; he inclined to me and heard my cry."

2. "He drew me up from the pit of destruction, out of the miry bog, and set my feet upon a rock, making my steps secure."

3. "He put a new song in my mouth, a song of praise to our God. Many will see and fear, and put their trust in the Lord."

By helping individuals create new, positive narratives about their lives, chaplains can support their journey toward healing and growth.

Chaplains employ a range of counseling techniques, such as cognitive-behavioral therapy, solution-focused therapy, and narrative therapy, to address specific issues and promote healing and growth. By utilizing these approaches, chaplains can effectively support individuals in navigating their challenges and finding paths to personal growth and healing. Through an exploration of biblical foundations, theological implications, and practical applications, we have gained a deeper understanding of these counseling techniques. As we continue to delve into pastoral care and counseling, the commitment to providing comprehensive support and promoting personal growth will remain central, guiding and informing the practice of chaplaincy.

Crisis Intervention

Crisis intervention is a critical aspect of chaplaincy, involving the provision of immediate support and stabilization in response to traumatic events, such as accidents, natural disasters, and personal crises. Effective crisis intervention can significantly impact individuals' ability to cope with and recover from traumatic experiences. This chapter explores the principles, methods, and applications of crisis intervention in chaplaincy, supported by biblical foundations, theological implications, and practical strategies.

Biblical Foundations of Crisis Intervention

The Bible provides numerous examples of crisis intervention, highlighting the importance of providing immediate support and stabilization during times of distress.

God as a Refuge

The Bible often portrays God as a refuge and source of strength in times of trouble.

Psalm 46:1 (ESV):

1. "God is our refuge and strength, a very present help in trouble."

This verse emphasizes the importance of seeking and providing immediate support during crises, reflecting the role of chaplains in offering stability and strength.

Compassion and Support

Providing compassion and support during times of crisis is a key biblical principle.

Isaiah 41:10 (ESV):

10. "Fear not, for I am with you; be not dismayed, for I am your God; I will strengthen you, I will help you, I will uphold you with my righteous right hand."

This passage highlights God's promise of support and strength, which chaplains emulate in their crisis intervention efforts.

Theological Implications of Crisis Intervention

Crisis intervention reflects several important theological themes, including God's compassion, the presence of the Holy Spirit, and the call to bear one another's burdens.

Reflecting God's Compassion

Chaplains reflect God's compassion by providing immediate support to those in crisis.

2 Corinthians 1:3-4 (ESV):

3. "Blessed be the God and Father of our Lord Jesus Christ, the Father of mercies and God of all comfort,"

4. "who comforts us in all our affliction, so that we may be able to comfort those who are in any affliction, with the comfort with which we ourselves are comforted by God."

This passage emphasizes the role of believers in providing comfort to others, mirroring the comfort they receive from God.

The Presence of the Holy Spirit

The Holy Spirit's presence provides guidance and strength during times of crisis.

John 14:16-17 (ESV):

16. "And I will ask the Father, and he will give you another Helper, to be with you forever,"

17. "even the Spirit of truth, whom the world cannot receive because it neither sees him nor knows him. You know him, for he dwells with you and will be in you."

Chaplains, empowered by the Holy Spirit, offer guidance and support to individuals in crisis.

Bearing One Another's Burdens

The call to bear one another's burdens is central to the practice of crisis intervention.

Galatians 6:2 (ESV):

2. "Bear one another's burdens, and so fulfill the law of Christ."

By providing immediate support, chaplains help individuals carry their burdens during times of crisis.

Practical Applications of Crisis Intervention

Crisis intervention involves various practical applications, including providing emotional support, facilitating communication, and coordinating resources.

Providing Emotional Support

Emotional support is a critical component of crisis intervention, helping individuals manage their emotional reactions to traumatic events.

Romans 12:15 (ESV):

15. "Rejoice with those who rejoice, weep with those who weep."

By offering a compassionate presence and empathetic listening, chaplains help individuals feel understood and supported.

Facilitating Communication

Effective communication is essential during a crisis, helping to clarify information and reduce confusion.

Proverbs 15:1 (ESV):

1. "A soft answer turns away wrath, but a harsh word stirs up anger."

Chaplains facilitate clear and calm communication, helping individuals process information and make informed decisions.

Coordinating Resources

Chaplains coordinate resources to meet the practical needs of individuals in crisis, ensuring they receive appropriate care and support.

Acts 6:3 (ESV):

3. "Therefore, brothers, pick out from among you seven men of good repute, full of the Spirit and of wisdom, whom we will appoint to this duty."

By coordinating resources and support, chaplains help individuals access the help they need to navigate their crisis.

Expository Study with Exhaustive Strong's Concordance

To deepen our understanding of crisis intervention, we turn to Strong's Exhaustive Concordance to explore key Hebrew and Greek terms.

Help and Support

- Hebrew: "Ezrah" (עֶזְרָה, Strong's H5833): This term means help or support, underscoring the assistance provided during crisis intervention (Psalm 46:1).

- Greek: "Boetheia" (βοήθεια, Strong's G996): This term means help or aid, highlighting the support offered during crises (Hebrews 4:16).

Comfort

- Greek: "Paraklesis" (παράκλησις, Strong's G3874): This term means comfort or encouragement, emphasizing the role of providing solace during crises (2 Corinthians 1:3-4).

Comprehensive Commentary

Providing Immediate Support and Stabilization

The biblical concept of providing immediate support and stabilization is central to crisis intervention. The Hebrew term "ezrah" (Strong's H5833) and the Greek term "boetheia" (Strong's G996) both emphasize the importance of offering help and support during times of distress. Chaplains, by providing immediate support, help individuals manage their emotional reactions and stabilize their situation.

Offering Comfort and Encouragement

Comfort and encouragement are essential components of crisis intervention. The Greek term "paraklesis" (Strong's G3874) underscores the importance of providing solace and support during crises. Chaplains, by offering comfort and encouragement, help individuals find strength and hope in the midst of their distress.

Practical Examples of Crisis Intervention in Chaplaincy

Responding to Accidents and Natural Disasters

Chaplains provide immediate support and stabilization in the aftermath of accidents and natural disasters, offering emotional support, facilitating communication, and coordinating resources.

Psalm 46:1 (ESV):

1. "God is our refuge and strength, a very present help in trouble."

By acting as a stabilizing presence, chaplains help individuals navigate the chaos and uncertainty of traumatic events.

Supporting Individuals During Personal Crises

Chaplains support individuals experiencing personal crises, such as the loss of a loved one, job loss, or relationship breakdown, offering empathetic listening and practical assistance.

Romans 12:15 (ESV):

15. "Rejoice with those who rejoice, weep with those who weep."

By providing compassionate support, chaplains help individuals cope with their emotional distress and find a path forward.

Facilitating Communication and Coordination

Chaplains facilitate communication and coordinate resources during crises, ensuring that individuals receive accurate information and appropriate support.

Proverbs 15:1 (ESV):

1. "A soft answer turns away wrath, but a harsh word stirs up anger."

By promoting clear and calm communication, chaplains help reduce confusion and support effective decision-making.

Crisis intervention is a critical aspect of chaplaincy, involving providing immediate support and stabilization in response to traumatic events, such as accidents, natural disasters, and personal crises. By offering emotional support, facilitating communication, and coordinating resources, chaplains play a vital role in helping individuals navigate and recover from crises. Through an exploration of biblical foundations, theological implications, and practical applications, we have gained a deeper understanding of the principles and practices of crisis intervention. As we continue to delve into pastoral care and counseling, the commitment to providing compassionate and effective crisis intervention will remain central, guiding and informing the practice of chaplaincy.

CHAPTER 07

ETHICAL CHALLENGES IN CHAPLAINCY

Confidentiality

Maintaining confidentiality is a fundamental ethical principle in chaplaincy, requiring chaplains to protect the privacy of those they serve while balancing legal and organizational obligations. Confidentiality is crucial for building trust, fostering open communication, and ensuring the ethical integrity of the chaplain's ministry. This chapter explores the importance of confidentiality in chaplaincy, the biblical and theological foundations for maintaining confidentiality, and practical strategies for managing confidentiality in various settings.

Importance of Confidentiality in Chaplaincy

Confidentiality is essential in chaplaincy for several reasons:

1. Building Trust: Confidentiality helps build trust between chaplains and those they serve. When individuals feel confident that their private information will be protected, they are more likely to share openly and honestly.

2. Encouraging Open Communication: Maintaining confidentiality encourages individuals to communicate openly about their concerns, struggles, and spiritual needs, allowing chaplains to provide more effective support.

3. Ensuring Ethical Integrity: Adhering to confidentiality standards helps maintain the ethical integrity of the chaplaincy profession and fosters a culture of respect and trust within organizations.

Biblical and Theological Foundations for Confidentiality

The Bible provides several principles that support the practice of confidentiality in chaplaincy.

Respecting Privacy and Dignity

The Bible emphasizes the importance of respecting the privacy and dignity of others.

Proverbs 11:13 (ESV):

13. "Whoever goes about slandering reveals secrets, but he who is trustworthy in spirit keeps a thing covered."

This verse underscores the value of discretion and trustworthiness, which are essential for maintaining confidentiality.

Bearing One Another's Burdens

Confidentiality is integral to the biblical principle of bearing one another's burdens.

Galatians 6:2 (ESV):

2. "Bear one another's burdens, and so fulfill the law of Christ."

By keeping confidential information private, chaplains honor the trust placed in them and provide a safe space for individuals to share their burdens.

The Role of the Shepherd

The role of the shepherd in the Bible includes protecting the flock, which can be extended to protecting the privacy of those under a chaplain's care.

John 10:14 (ESV):

14. "I am the good shepherd. I know my own and my own know me."

Chaplains, as spiritual shepherds, are called to protect the confidentiality of those they serve, ensuring their well-being and trust.

Practical Strategies for Managing Confidentiality

Chaplains can employ various strategies to manage confidentiality effectively in different settings.

Understanding Legal and Organizational Requirements

Chaplains must be aware of the legal and organizational requirements related to confidentiality in their specific context. This includes understanding mandatory reporting laws, organizational policies, and professional ethical guidelines.

Romans 13:1 (ESV):

1. "Let every person be subject to the governing authorities. For there is no authority except from God, and those that exist have been instituted by God."

By complying with legal and organizational requirements, chaplains can navigate the complexities of confidentiality while upholding ethical standards.

Establishing Clear Boundaries

Establishing clear boundaries with individuals about the limits of confidentiality is crucial. Chaplains should communicate these boundaries at the outset of their interactions, ensuring that individuals understand the conditions under which confidentiality might be breached (e.g., risk of harm to self or others).

Matthew 5:37 (ESV):

37. "Let what you say be simply 'Yes' or 'No'; anything more than this comes from evil."

Clear communication about confidentiality boundaries helps prevent misunderstandings and fosters trust.

Creating a Safe Environment

Chaplains should create a safe and private environment for conversations, ensuring that individuals feel secure in sharing sensitive information.

Psalm 91:1 (ESV):

1. "He who dwells in the shelter of the Most High will abide in the shadow of the Almighty."

Providing a private and secure setting for discussions reinforces the commitment to confidentiality and builds trust.

Handling Confidential Information

Chaplains must handle confidential information with care, storing records securely and limiting access to authorized personnel only.

Proverbs 2:11 (ESV):

11. "Discretion will watch over you, understanding will guard you."

By practicing discretion and careful handling of information, chaplains can protect the privacy of those they serve.

Expository Study with Exhaustive Strong's Concordance

To deepen our understanding of confidentiality, we turn to Strong's Exhaustive Concordance to explore key Hebrew and Greek terms.

Trust and Discretion

- Hebrew: "Emunah" (אֱמוּנָה, Strong's H530): This term means faithfulness or trust, underscoring the importance of trust in maintaining confidentiality (Proverbs 11:13).

- Greek: "Pistis" (πίστις, Strong's G4102): This term means faith or trust, highlighting the role of trust in the chaplaincy relationship (Galatians 6:2).

Comprehensive Commentary

Building Trust Through Confidentiality

The biblical concepts of faithfulness and trust are central to the practice of confidentiality. The Hebrew term "emunah" (Strong's H530) and the Greek term "pistis" (Strong's G4102) both emphasize the importance of trust in relationships. Chaplains, by maintaining confidentiality, build trust and create a safe space for individuals to share their struggles and receive support.

Protecting Privacy and Dignity

Respecting privacy and dignity is a fundamental aspect of chaplaincy. The biblical principle of discretion, as highlighted in Proverbs 11:13, underscores the importance of keeping sensitive information private. Chaplains, by practicing discretion, honor the dignity of those they serve and maintain the ethical integrity of their ministry.

Practical Examples of Maintaining Confidentiality in Chaplaincy

In Healthcare Settings

In healthcare settings, chaplains must navigate complex confidentiality requirements, including patient privacy laws (e.g., HIPAA in the United States). They should ensure that patient information is shared only with authorized personnel and that conversations with patients are conducted in private settings.

Romans 13:1 (ESV):

1. "Let every person be subject to the governing authorities. For there is no authority except from God, and those that exist have been instituted by God."

By complying with legal requirements and organizational policies, chaplains protect patient privacy and maintain trust.

In Military Settings

In military settings, chaplains may encounter situations where confidentiality must be balanced with the need to report potential threats to safety. They should establish clear boundaries with service members about the limits of confidentiality and provide support within those boundaries.

Matthew 5:37 (ESV):

37. "Let what you say be simply 'Yes' or 'No'; anything more than this comes from evil."

Clear communication about confidentiality boundaries helps prevent misunderstandings and fosters trust in the chaplaincy relationship.

In Corporate Settings

In corporate settings, chaplains may support employees facing personal or professional challenges. They should ensure that confidential information shared by employees is kept private and only disclosed when absolutely necessary, in accordance with organizational policies.

Proverbs 2:11 (ESV):

11. "Discretion will watch over you, understanding will guard you."

By practicing discretion and careful handling of information, chaplains protect employee privacy and maintain a trustworthy environment.

Maintaining confidentiality is a fundamental ethical principle in chaplaincy, requiring chaplains to protect the privacy of those they serve while balancing legal and organizational obligations. By building trust, encouraging open communication, and ensuring ethical integrity, chaplains create a safe space for individuals to share their struggles and receive support. Through an exploration of biblical and theological foundations, practical strategies, and key terms, we have gained a deeper understanding of the importance and practice of confidentiality in chaplaincy. As we continue to navigate ethical challenges in chaplaincy, the commitment to maintaining confidentiality will remain central, guiding and informing the practice of chaplaincy in various settings.

Boundaries

Establishing and maintaining appropriate boundaries is essential for ethical chaplaincy practice, ensuring that chaplains provide care without becoming overly involved or crossing professional lines. Boundaries help protect both the chaplains and those they serve, promoting a healthy and respectful relationship. This chapter explores the importance of boundaries in chaplaincy, the biblical and theological foundations for boundary-setting, and practical strategies for maintaining boundaries in various contexts.

Importance of Boundaries in Chaplaincy

Boundaries are crucial in chaplaincy for several reasons:

1. Promoting Professionalism: Boundaries help maintain a professional relationship between chaplains and those they serve, ensuring that care is provided in a respectful and ethical manner.

2. Protecting Both Parties: Boundaries protect chaplains from becoming overly involved in the personal lives of those they serve, and they protect individuals from potential exploitation or harm.

3. Enhancing Effectiveness: Clear boundaries allow chaplains to focus on their primary role of providing spiritual and emotional support without becoming entangled in personal or organizational issues.

Biblical and Theological Foundations for Boundary-Setting

The Bible provides several principles that support the practice of setting and maintaining boundaries.

Respecting Personal Space

The Bible emphasizes the importance of respecting personal space and boundaries.

Proverbs 25:17 (ESV):

17. "Let your foot be seldom in your neighbor's house, lest he have his fill of you and hate you."

This verse highlights the importance of respecting others' space and avoiding overstepping boundaries.

Guarding the Heart

Setting boundaries is a way to guard one's heart and maintain spiritual and emotional well-being.

Proverbs 4:23 (ESV):

23. "Keep your heart with all vigilance, for from it flow the springs of life."

Chaplains must guard their hearts by setting boundaries that protect their emotional and spiritual health.

The Role of Shepherds

The role of shepherds in the Bible includes setting boundaries to protect the flock and ensure their well-being.

John 10:11-13 (ESV):

11. "I am the good shepherd. The good shepherd lays down his life for the sheep."

12. "He who is a hired hand and not a shepherd, who does not own the sheep, sees the wolf coming and leaves the sheep and flees, and the wolf snatches them and scatters them."

13. "He flees because he is a hired hand and cares nothing for the sheep."

Chaplains, as spiritual shepherds, set boundaries to protect those they serve and provide effective care.

Practical Strategies for Maintaining Boundaries

Chaplains can employ various strategies to maintain appropriate boundaries in their practice.

Clear Communication

Clear communication about boundaries is essential from the outset of the chaplaincy relationship. Chaplains should explain the scope of their role and the limits of their involvement.

Matthew 5:37 (ESV):

37. "Let what you say be simply 'Yes' or 'No'; anything more than this comes from evil."

By communicating clearly, chaplains help prevent misunderstandings and set expectations.

Self-Awareness and Reflection

Chaplains must be self-aware and reflect on their own motivations and emotional responses. This self-awareness helps identify when boundaries may be at risk of being crossed.

Psalm 139:23-24 (ESV):

23. "Search me, O God, and know my heart! Try me and know my thoughts!"

24. "And see if there be any grievous way in me, and lead me in the way everlasting!"

Regular self-reflection allows chaplains to maintain healthy boundaries and address any personal issues that may arise.

Supervision and Accountability

Supervision and accountability are crucial for maintaining boundaries. Regular meetings with a supervisor or mentor can provide support and guidance in managing boundaries.

Proverbs 11:14 (ESV):

14. "Where there is no guidance, a people falls, but in an abundance of counselors there is safety."

Having a support system in place helps chaplains navigate boundary challenges and maintain ethical practice.

Time Management

Effective time management helps chaplains set boundaries around their availability and prevent burnout. This includes setting limits on work hours and ensuring time for personal rest and renewal.

Exodus 20:8-10 (ESV):

8. "Remember the Sabbath day, to keep it holy."

9. "Six days you shall labor, and do all your work,"

10. "but the seventh day is a Sabbath to the Lord your God. On it you shall not do any work, you, or your son, or

your daughter, your male servant, or your female servant, or your livestock, or the sojourner who is within your gates."

By managing their time effectively, chaplains can maintain boundaries that protect their well-being and effectiveness.

Expository Study with Exhaustive Strong's Concordance

To deepen our understanding of boundaries, we turn to Strong's Exhaustive Concordance to explore key Hebrew and Greek terms.

Guarding and Protecting

- Hebrew: "Shamar" (שָׁמַר, Strong's H8104): This term means to guard, keep, or protect, reflecting the role of boundaries in safeguarding well-being (Proverbs 4:23).

- Greek: "Phylasso" (φυλάσσω, Strong's G5442): This term means to guard or watch, emphasizing the importance of protecting boundaries (2 Timothy 1:14).

Comprehensive Commentary

Respecting Personal Space and Boundaries

The biblical concepts of guarding and protecting are central to the practice of boundary-setting. The Hebrew term "shamar" (Strong's H8104) and the Greek term "phylasso" (Strong's G5442) both emphasize the importance of safeguarding well-being. Chaplains, by setting and maintaining boundaries, protect their own well-being and that of those they serve.

Clear Communication and Accountability

Clear communication and accountability are essential components of ethical chaplaincy practice. The biblical principle of honesty, as highlighted in Matthew 5:37, underscores the importance of transparent communication. By clearly communicating boundaries and seeking accountability, chaplains maintain ethical integrity and foster trust.

Practical Examples of Maintaining Boundaries in Chaplaincy

In Healthcare Settings

In healthcare settings, chaplains must navigate complex relationships with patients, families, and medical staff. They should set clear boundaries regarding their role and availability, and ensure they do not become overly involved in medical decisions or personal relationships.

Proverbs 4:23 (ESV):

23. "Keep your heart with all vigilance, for from it flow the springs of life."

By maintaining boundaries, chaplains protect their emotional and spiritual well-being while providing effective care.

In Military Settings

In military settings, chaplains may face unique boundary challenges due to the close-knit nature of military communities. They should establish clear professional boundaries while providing support to service members and their families.

Psalm 139:23-24 (ESV):

23. "Search me, O God, and know my heart! Try me and know my thoughts!"

24. "And see if there be any grievous way in me, and lead me in the way everlasting!"

Regular self-reflection and supervision help chaplains navigate these challenges and maintain ethical practice.

In Corporate Settings

In corporate settings, chaplains must balance their pastoral role with the organizational culture and dynamics. They should set boundaries around their involvement in workplace issues and maintain a professional distance from employees' personal lives.

Matthew 5:37 (ESV):

37. "Let what you say be simply 'Yes' or 'No'; anything more than this comes from evil."

Clear communication about boundaries helps prevent misunderstandings and fosters a professional relationship with employees.

Establishing and maintaining appropriate boundaries is essential for ethical chaplaincy practice, ensuring that chaplains provide care without becoming overly involved or crossing professional lines. By promoting professionalism, protecting both parties, and enhancing effectiveness, boundaries help chaplains fulfill their role in a respectful and ethical manner. Through an exploration of biblical and theological foundations, practical strategies, and key terms, we have gained a deeper understanding of the importance and practice of boundary-setting in chaplaincy. As we continue to navigate ethical challenges in chaplaincy, the commitment to maintaining boundaries will remain central, guiding and informing the practice of chaplaincy in various settings.

Cultural Competence

Cultural competence involves understanding and respecting the diverse backgrounds and beliefs of those served by chaplains, ensuring that care is inclusive and sensitive to individual needs. This chapter explores the importance of cultural competence in chaplaincy, the biblical and theological foundations for respecting diversity, and practical strategies for providing culturally sensitive care in various contexts.

Importance of Cultural Competence in Chaplaincy

Cultural competence is crucial in chaplaincy for several reasons:

1. Fostering Inclusivity: Cultural competence helps create an inclusive environment where individuals from diverse backgrounds feel respected and valued.

2. Enhancing Communication: Understanding cultural differences enhances communication, enabling chaplains to connect more effectively with those they serve.

3. Improving Care: Culturally competent care addresses the unique needs and preferences of individuals, leading to more effective and personalized support.

Biblical and Theological Foundations for Cultural Competence

The Bible provides several principles that support the practice of cultural competence in chaplaincy.

Respecting All People

The Bible emphasizes the importance of respecting and valuing all people, regardless of their background.

Genesis 1:27 (ESV):

27. "So God created man in his own image, in the image of God he created him; male and female he created them."

This verse highlights the inherent dignity and worth of every person, created in the image of God.

Loving Our Neighbor

The command to love our neighbor is central to the Christian faith and includes respecting and valuing cultural differences.

Mark 12:31 (ESV):

31. "The second is this: 'You shall love your neighbor as yourself.' There is no other commandment greater than these."

Loving our neighbor involves understanding and respecting their cultural background and beliefs.

Embracing Diversity

The Bible celebrates diversity and the inclusion of people from all nations and backgrounds in God's plan.

Revelation 7:9 (ESV):

9. "After this I looked, and behold, a great multitude that no one could number, from every nation, from all tribes and peoples and languages, standing before the throne and before the Lamb, clothed in white robes, with palm branches in their hands."

This vision of a diverse multitude worshiping together underscores the value of cultural diversity.

Practical Strategies for Providing Culturally Sensitive Care

Chaplains can employ various strategies to provide culturally sensitive care in their practice.

Educating Themselves

Chaplains should educate themselves about the cultural backgrounds and beliefs of those they serve. This includes learning about different religious practices, customs, and values.

Proverbs 4:7 (ESV):

7. "The beginning of wisdom is this: Get wisdom, and whatever you get, get insight."

By seeking knowledge and understanding, chaplains can provide more effective and respectful care.

Practicing Active Listening

Active listening involves paying close attention to individuals' words and non-verbal cues, demonstrating respect and openness to their experiences and perspectives.

James 1:19 (ESV):

19. "Know this, my beloved brothers: let every person be quick to hear, slow to speak, slow to anger."

By practicing active listening, chaplains show respect for individuals' cultural backgrounds and build trust.

Avoiding Assumptions

Chaplains should avoid making assumptions about individuals based on their cultural background. Instead, they should seek to understand each person's unique experiences and perspectives.

Proverbs 18:13 (ESV):

13. "If one gives an answer before he hears, it is his folly and shame."

By avoiding assumptions, chaplains can provide more personalized and respectful care.

Collaborating with Cultural Brokers

In some cases, chaplains may benefit from collaborating with cultural brokers—individuals who have a deep understanding of a particular culture and can help bridge cultural gaps.

Proverbs 15:22 (ESV):

22. "Without counsel plans fail, but with many advisers they succeed."

Collaborating with cultural brokers can enhance chaplains' understanding and effectiveness in providing culturally competent care.

Expository Study with Exhaustive Strong's Concordance

To deepen our understanding of cultural competence, we turn to Strong's Exhaustive Concordance to explore key Hebrew and Greek terms.

Respect and Value

- Hebrew: "Kabad" (כָּבַד, Strong's H3513): This term means to honor or respect, underscoring the importance of valuing all people (Exodus 20:12).

- Greek: "Timao" (τιμάω, Strong's G5091): This term means to honor or value, highlighting the respect we should have for others (1 Peter 2:17).

Diversity and Inclusion

- Greek: "Polupoikilos" (πολυποίκιλος, Strong's G4182): This term means manifold or diverse, reflecting the richness of cultural diversity (Ephesians 3:10).

Comprehensive Commentary

Respecting and Valuing Diversity

The biblical concepts of honor and respect are central to cultural competence. The Hebrew term "kabad" (Strong's H3513) and the Greek term "timao" (Strong's G5091) both emphasize the importance of valuing and respecting all people. Chaplains, by honoring the cultural backgrounds and beliefs of those they serve, foster an inclusive and respectful environment.

Celebrating Cultural Diversity

The Bible celebrates cultural diversity and inclusion, as reflected in the vision of a diverse multitude worshiping together in Revelation 7:9. The Greek term "polupoikilos" (Strong's G4182) underscores the richness and value of diversity. Chaplains, by embracing and celebrating cultural diversity, reflect the inclusive nature of God's kingdom.

Practical Examples of Cultural Competence in Chaplaincy

In Healthcare Settings

In healthcare settings, chaplains may serve patients from diverse cultural backgrounds. They should educate themselves about different cultural practices related to health, illness, and end-of-life care.

Proverbs 4:7 (ESV):

7. "The beginning of wisdom is this: Get wisdom, and whatever you get, get insight."

By seeking knowledge and understanding, chaplains can provide more effective and respectful care.

In Military Settings

In military settings, chaplains may work with service members from various cultural and religious backgrounds.

They should practice active listening and avoid assumptions to build trust and provide personalized support.

James 1:19 (ESV):

19. "Know this, my beloved brothers: let every person be quick to hear, slow to speak, slow to anger."

By demonstrating respect and openness, chaplains can effectively support service members' spiritual and emotional needs.

In Corporate Settings

In corporate settings, chaplains may support employees from diverse cultural backgrounds. They should collaborate with cultural brokers and seek to understand the unique experiences and perspectives of each employee.

Proverbs 15:22 (ESV):

22. "Without counsel plans fail, but with many advisers they succeed."

By working with cultural brokers, chaplains can enhance their understanding and effectiveness in providing culturally competent care.

Cultural competence involves understanding and respecting the diverse backgrounds and beliefs of those served by chaplains, ensuring that care is inclusive and sensitive to individual needs. By fostering inclusivity, enhancing communication, and improving care, cultural competence helps chaplains provide effective and respectful support. Through an exploration of biblical and theological foundations, practical strategies, and key terms, we have gained a deeper understanding of the importance and practice of cultural competence in chaplaincy. As we continue to navigate ethical challenges in chaplaincy, the commitment to cultural competence will remain central, guiding and informing the practice of chaplaincy in various settings.

CHAPTER 08

INTERFAITH CHAPLAINCY

The Role of Interfaith Chaplains

Interfaith chaplains provide spiritual care to individuals from a variety of religious and spiritual traditions, fostering mutual understanding and respect. In an increasingly diverse and pluralistic world, interfaith chaplains play a crucial role in bridging religious divides, promoting harmony, and supporting the spiritual needs of diverse communities. This chapter explores the role of interfaith chaplains, the biblical and theological foundations for interfaith ministry, and practical strategies for effectively serving individuals from different faith traditions.

Importance of Interfaith Chaplaincy

Interfaith chaplaincy is important for several reasons:

1. Promoting Inclusivity: Interfaith chaplains create an inclusive environment where individuals of all faiths feel respected and valued.

2. Fostering Mutual Understanding: By engaging with diverse religious traditions, interfaith chaplains foster mutual understanding and respect.

3. Addressing Diverse Spiritual Needs: Interfaith chaplains are equipped to address the spiritual needs of individuals from various religious backgrounds, providing appropriate and sensitive care.

Biblical and Theological Foundations for Interfaith Ministry

The Bible and theological principles provide a foundation for interfaith ministry, emphasizing respect, love, and the recognition of common humanity.

Respecting All People

The Bible teaches the importance of respecting and valuing all people, regardless of their faith background.

Genesis 1:27 (ESV):

27. "So God created man in his own image, in the image of God he created him; male and female he created them."

This verse underscores the inherent dignity and worth of every person, created in the image of God.

Loving Our Neighbor

The command to love our neighbor includes showing respect and kindness to individuals of different faiths.

Mark 12:31 (ESV):

31. "The second is this: 'You shall love your neighbor as yourself.' There is no other commandment greater than these."

Loving our neighbor involves understanding and respecting their religious beliefs and practices.

Peace and Reconciliation

The Bible calls for peace and reconciliation, which can be extended to interfaith relationships.

Romans 12:18 (ESV):

18. "If possible, so far as it depends on you, live peaceably with all."

Chaplains are called to be peacemakers, fostering harmony and understanding among people of different faiths.

Practical Strategies for Interfaith Chaplaincy

Interfaith chaplains can employ various strategies to effectively serve individuals from diverse religious traditions.

Education and Training

Interfaith chaplains should educate themselves about the beliefs, practices, and traditions of various religions. This includes formal education, attending interfaith events, and engaging in dialogue with individuals from different faith backgrounds.

Proverbs 4:7 (ESV):

7. "The beginning of wisdom is this: Get wisdom, and whatever you get, get insight."

By seeking knowledge and understanding, chaplains can provide more respectful and effective care.

Building Relationships

Building relationships with individuals from different faith traditions is crucial for effective interfaith chaplaincy. This involves active listening, empathy, and showing genuine interest in their beliefs and practices.

James 1:19 (ESV):

19. "Know this, my beloved brothers: let every person be quick to hear, slow to speak, slow to anger."

By practicing active listening and empathy, chaplains build trust and foster mutual understanding.

Facilitating Interfaith Dialogue

Interfaith chaplains can facilitate dialogue between individuals of different faiths, promoting mutual understanding and respect. This can include organizing interfaith events, discussion groups, and collaborative projects.

Ephesians 4:2-3 (ESV):

2. "With all humility and gentleness, with patience, bearing with one another in love,"

3. "eager to maintain the unity of the Spirit in the bond of peace."

By promoting dialogue and collaboration, chaplains foster a spirit of unity and peace.

Providing Inclusive Spiritual Care

Interfaith chaplains provide spiritual care that respects and honors the diverse religious beliefs and practices of those they serve. This includes being mindful of religious sensitivities, dietary restrictions, and prayer practices.

1 Corinthians 9:22 (ESV):

22. "To the weak I became weak, that I might win the weak. I have become all things to all people, that by all means I might save some."

By adapting their approach to meet the needs of individuals from different faiths, chaplains provide inclusive and respectful care.

Expository Study with Exhaustive Strong's Concordance

To deepen our understanding of interfaith chaplaincy, we turn to Strong's Exhaustive Concordance to explore key Hebrew and Greek terms.

Respect and Love

- Hebrew: "Kabad" (כָּבַד, Strong's H3513): This term means to honor or respect, underscoring the importance of valuing all people (Exodus 20:12).

- Greek: "Agapao" (ἀγαπάω, Strong's G25): This term means to love, emphasizing the command to love our neighbor (Mark 12:31).

Peace and Unity

- Greek: "Eirene" (εἰρήνη, Strong's G1515): This term means peace, reflecting the call to live peaceably with all (Romans 12:18).

- Greek: "Henotes" (ἑνότης, Strong's G1775): This term means unity, highlighting the importance of maintaining unity in the Spirit (Ephesians 4:3).

Comprehensive Commentary

Respecting and Valuing Diversity

The biblical concepts of honor and love are central to interfaith chaplaincy. The Hebrew term "kabad" (Strong's H3513) and the Greek term "agapao" (Strong's G25) both emphasize the importance of respecting and valuing all people. Chaplains, by honoring the diverse religious beliefs and practices of those they serve, foster an inclusive and respectful environment.

Promoting Peace and Unity

The call to peace and unity is essential for interfaith chaplaincy. The Greek term "eirene" (Strong's G1515) and the Greek term "henotes" (Strong's G1775) both highlight the importance of living peaceably and maintaining unity. Chaplains, by promoting interfaith dialogue and collaboration, contribute to a spirit of harmony and understanding.

Practical Examples of Interfaith Chaplaincy

In Healthcare Settings

In healthcare settings, interfaith chaplains may serve patients from diverse religious backgrounds. They should be knowledgeable about different religious practices related to health, illness, and end-of-life care.

Proverbs 4:7 (ESV):

7. "The beginning of wisdom is this: Get wisdom, and whatever you get, get insight."

By seeking knowledge and understanding, chaplains can provide more effective and respectful care.

In Military Settings

In military settings, interfaith chaplains may work with service members from various faith traditions. They should practice active listening and empathy to build trust and provide personalized support.

James 1:19 (ESV):

19. "Know this, my beloved brothers: let every person be quick to hear, slow to speak, slow to anger."

By demonstrating respect and openness, chaplains can effectively support service members' spiritual and emotional needs.

In Corporate Settings

In corporate settings, interfaith chaplains may support employees from diverse religious backgrounds. They should facilitate interfaith dialogue and provide inclusive spiritual care.

Ephesians 4:2-3 (ESV):

2. "With all humility and gentleness, with patience, bearing with one another in love,"

3. "eager to maintain the unity of the Spirit in the bond of peace."

By promoting dialogue and collaboration, chaplains foster a spirit of unity and respect in the workplace.

Interfaith chaplains provide spiritual care to individuals from a variety of religious and spiritual traditions, fostering mutual understanding and respect. By promoting inclusivity, fostering mutual understanding, and addressing diverse spiritual needs, interfaith chaplains play a crucial role in bridging religious divides and supporting the spiritual needs of diverse communities. Through an exploration of biblical and theological foundations, practical strategies, and key terms, we have gained a deeper understanding of the importance and practice of interfaith chaplaincy. As we continue to navigate the challenges of interfaith ministry, the commitment to mutual respect, understanding, and inclusive care will remain central, guiding and informing the practice of chaplaincy in various settings.

Navigating Religious Diversity

Navigating religious diversity with sensitivity and respect is crucial for chaplains, as they recognize the unique beliefs and practices of different faith traditions and provide care that honors each individual's spiritual journey. In an increasingly pluralistic society, chaplains must be adept at understanding and engaging with diverse religious perspectives. This chapter explores the importance of navigating religious diversity, the biblical and theological foundations for respecting religious differences, and practical strategies for providing inclusive and respectful spiritual care.

Importance of Navigating Religious Diversity

Navigating religious diversity is essential for several reasons:

1. Promoting Inclusivity: Respecting diverse religious beliefs fosters an inclusive environment where individuals feel valued and respected.

2. Enhancing Communication: Understanding religious diversity enhances communication, allowing chaplains to connect more effectively with those they serve.

3. Providing Personalized Care: Recognizing and honoring different religious practices enables chaplains to provide personalized and appropriate spiritual care.

Biblical and Theological Foundations for Respecting Religious Differences

The Bible and theological principles provide a foundation for respecting religious diversity, emphasizing love, respect, and the recognition of common humanity.

Respecting All People

The Bible teaches the importance of respecting and valuing all people, regardless of their religious background.

Genesis 1:27 (ESV):

27. "So God created man in his own image, in the image of God he created him; male and female he created them."

This verse underscores the inherent dignity and worth of every person, created in the image of God.

Loving Our Neighbor

The command to love our neighbor includes showing respect and kindness to individuals of different faiths.

Mark 12:31 (ESV):

31. "The second is this: 'You shall love your neighbor as yourself.' There is no other commandment greater than these."

Loving our neighbor involves understanding and respecting their religious beliefs and practices.

Embracing Diversity

The Bible celebrates diversity and the inclusion of people from all nations and backgrounds in God's plan.

Revelation 7:9 (ESV):

9. "After this I looked, and behold, a great multitude that no one could number, from every nation, from all tribes and peoples and languages, standing before the throne and before the Lamb, clothed in white robes, with palm branches in their hands."

This vision of a diverse multitude worshiping together underscores the value of cultural and religious diversity.

Practical Strategies for Navigating Religious Diversity

Chaplains can employ various strategies to effectively navigate religious diversity in their practice.

Educating Themselves

Chaplains should educate themselves about the beliefs, practices, and traditions of various religions. This includes formal education, attending interfaith events, and engaging in dialogue with individuals from different faith backgrounds.

Proverbs 4:7 (ESV):

7. "The beginning of wisdom is this: Get wisdom, and whatever you get, get insight."

By seeking knowledge and understanding, chaplains can provide more respectful and effective care.

Practicing Active Listening

Active listening involves paying close attention to individuals' words and non-verbal cues, demonstrating respect and openness to their experiences and perspectives.

James 1:19 (ESV):

19. "Know this, my beloved brothers: let every person be quick to hear, slow to speak, slow to anger."

By practicing active listening, chaplains show respect for individuals' religious backgrounds and build trust.

Avoiding Assumptions

Chaplains should avoid making assumptions about individuals based on their religious background. Instead, they should seek to understand each person's unique experiences and perspectives.

Proverbs 18:13 (ESV):

13. "If one gives an answer before he hears, it is his folly and shame."

By avoiding assumptions, chaplains can provide more personalized and respectful care.

Collaborating with Religious Leaders

In some cases, chaplains may benefit from collaborating with religious leaders from different faith traditions to better understand and support the individuals they serve.

Proverbs 15:22 (ESV):

22. "Without counsel plans fail, but with many advisers, they succeed."

Collaborating with religious leaders can enhance chaplains' understanding and effectiveness in providing culturally competent care.

Providing Inclusive Spiritual Care

Chaplains provide spiritual care that respects and honors the diverse religious beliefs and practices of those they serve. This includes being mindful of religious sensitivities, dietary restrictions, and prayer practices.

1 Corinthians 9:22 (ESV):

22. "To the weak I became weak, that I might win the weak. I have become all things to all people, that by all means I might save some."

By adapting their approach to meet the needs of individuals from different faiths, chaplains provide inclusive and respectful care.

Expository Study with Exhaustive Strong's Concordance

To deepen our understanding of navigating religious diversity, we turn to Strong's Exhaustive Concordance to explore key Hebrew and Greek terms.

Respect and Value

- Hebrew: "Kabad" (כָּבַד, Strong's H3513): This term means to honor or respect, underscoring the importance of valuing all people (Exodus 20:12).

- Greek: "Timao" (τιμάω, Strong's G5091): This term means to honor or value, highlighting the respect we should have for others (1 Peter 2:17).

Diversity and Inclusion

- Greek: "Polupoikilos" (πολυποίκιλος, Strong's G4182): This term means manifold or diverse, reflecting the richness of cultural and religious diversity (Ephesians 3:10).

Comprehensive Commentary

Respecting and Valuing Diversity

The biblical concepts of honor and respect are central to navigating religious diversity. The Hebrew term "kabad" (Strong's H3513) and the Greek term "timao" (Strong's

G5091) both emphasize the importance of valuing and respecting all people. Chaplains, by honoring the diverse religious beliefs and practices of those they serve, foster an inclusive and respectful environment.

Celebrating Religious Diversity

The Bible celebrates cultural and religious diversity, as reflected in the vision of a diverse multitude worshiping together in Revelation 7:9. The Greek term "polupoikilos" (Strong's G4182) underscores the richness and value of diversity. Chaplains, by embracing and celebrating religious diversity, reflect the inclusive nature of God's kingdom.

Practical Examples of Navigating Religious Diversity in Chaplaincy

In Healthcare Settings

In healthcare settings, chaplains may serve patients from diverse religious backgrounds. They should be knowledgeable about different religious practices related to health, illness, and end-of-life care.

Proverbs 4:7 (ESV):

7. "The beginning of wisdom is this: Get wisdom, and whatever you get, get insight."

By seeking knowledge and understanding, chaplains can provide more effective and respectful care.

In Military Settings

In military settings, chaplains may work with service members from various religious backgrounds. They should practice active listening and empathy to build trust and provide personalized support.

James 1:19 (ESV):

19. "Know this, my beloved brothers: let every person be quick to hear, slow to speak, slow to anger."

By demonstrating respect and openness, chaplains can effectively support service members' spiritual and emotional needs.

In Corporate Settings

In corporate settings, chaplains may support employees from diverse religious backgrounds. They should facilitate interfaith dialogue and provide inclusive spiritual care.

Ephesians 4:2-3 (ESV):

2. "With all humility and gentleness, with patience, bearing with one another in love,"

3. "eager to maintain the unity of the Spirit in the bond of peace."

By promoting dialogue and collaboration, chaplains foster a spirit of unity and respect in the workplace.

Navigating religious diversity with sensitivity and respect is crucial for chaplains, as they recognize the unique beliefs and practices of different faith traditions and provide care that honors each individual's spiritual journey. By promoting inclusivity, enhancing communication, and providing personalized care, chaplains play a vital role in supporting the spiritual needs of diverse communities. Through an exploration of biblical and theological foundations, practical strategies, and key terms, we have gained a deeper understanding of the importance and practice of navigating religious diversity in chaplaincy. As we continue to navigate the challenges of interfaith ministry, the commitment to mutual respect, understanding, and inclusive care will remain central, guiding and informing the practice of chaplaincy in various settings.

Promoting Interfaith Dialogue

Interfaith chaplains play a crucial role in promoting dialogue and understanding between different religious communities, fostering a spirit of cooperation and mutual respect. In a world where religious diversity is increasingly prevalent, interfaith dialogue helps to build bridges, reduce misunderstandings, and promote peace. This chapter explores the importance of interfaith dialogue, the biblical and theological foundations for fostering such dialogue, and practical strategies for effectively promoting interfaith conversations and cooperation.

Importance of Interfaith Dialogue

Interfaith dialogue is essential for several reasons:

1. Building Bridges: Dialogue helps to build bridges between different religious communities, fostering mutual understanding and respect.

2. Reducing Misunderstandings: By engaging in open and honest conversations, individuals can dispel myths and misunderstandings about different faith traditions.

3. Promoting Peace: Interfaith dialogue promotes peace and cooperation, helping to address conflicts and promote harmony in diverse communities.

4. Enhancing Spiritual Growth: Engaging with diverse religious perspectives can enrich individuals' spiritual growth and understanding.

Biblical and Theological Foundations for Interfaith Dialogue

The Bible and theological principles provide a foundation for promoting interfaith dialogue, emphasizing love, respect, and the recognition of common humanity.

Respecting All People

The Bible teaches the importance of respecting and valuing all people, regardless of their religious background.

Genesis 1:27 (ESV):

27. "So God created man in his own image, in the image of God he created him; male and female he created them."

This verse underscores the inherent dignity and worth of every person, created in the image of God.

Loving Our Neighbor

The command to love our neighbor includes showing respect and kindness to individuals of different faiths.

Mark 12:31 (ESV):

31. "The second is this: 'You shall love your neighbor as yourself.' There is no other commandment greater than these."

Loving our neighbor involves understanding and respecting their religious beliefs and practices.

Pursuing Peace and Reconciliation

The Bible calls for peace and reconciliation, which can be extended to interfaith relationships.

Romans 12:18 (ESV):

18. "If possible, so far as it depends on you, live peaceably with all."

Chaplains are called to be peacemakers, fostering harmony and understanding among people of different faiths.

Practical Strategies for Promoting Interfaith Dialogue

Interfaith chaplains can employ various strategies to effectively promote dialogue and cooperation between different religious communities.

Education and Awareness

Interfaith chaplains should educate themselves and others about the beliefs, practices, and traditions of various religions. This includes organizing educational events, workshops, and seminars that foster understanding and respect.

Proverbs 4:7 (ESV):

7. "The beginning of wisdom is this: Get wisdom, and whatever you get, get insight."

By seeking knowledge and understanding, chaplains can help dispel myths and promote respect for diverse religious traditions.

Facilitating Interfaith Events

Organizing and facilitating interfaith events, such as panel discussions, interfaith services, and community gatherings, provides opportunities for individuals to engage in dialogue and build relationships.

Ephesians 4:2-3 (ESV):

2. "With all humility and gentleness, with patience, bearing with one another in love,"

3. "eager to maintain the unity of the Spirit in the bond of peace."

By promoting dialogue and collaboration, chaplains foster a spirit of unity and peace.

Encouraging Open and Respectful Dialogue

Chaplains should encourage open and respectful dialogue by creating safe spaces where individuals can share their beliefs and experiences without fear of judgment or hostility.

James 1:19 (ESV):

19. "Know this, my beloved brothers: let every person be quick to hear, slow to speak, slow to anger."

By practicing active listening and empathy, chaplains create an environment conducive to meaningful dialogue.

Building Relationships with Religious Leaders

Building relationships with religious leaders from different faith traditions is crucial for promoting interfaith dialogue. Chaplains can collaborate with these leaders to organize joint initiatives and address common concerns.

Proverbs 15:22 (ESV):

22. "Without counsel plans fail, but with many advisers they succeed."

Collaborating with religious leaders enhances the effectiveness of interfaith efforts and promotes mutual respect.

Addressing Common Issues

Focusing on common issues and concerns, such as social justice, poverty, and peacebuilding, can unite individuals from different faith traditions and promote cooperation.

Micah 6:8 (ESV):

8. "He has told you, O man, what is good; and what does the Lord require of you but to do justice, and to love kindness, and to walk humbly with your God?"

By working together on shared goals, chaplains and religious communities can build stronger relationships and promote positive change.

Expository Study with Exhaustive Strong's Concordance

To deepen our understanding of promoting interfaith dialogue, we turn to Strong's Exhaustive Concordance to explore key Hebrew and Greek terms.

Respect and Love

- Hebrew: "Kabad" (כָּבַד, Strong's H3513): This term means to honor or respect, underscoring the importance of valuing all people (Exodus 20:12).

- Greek: "Agapao" (ἀγαπάω, Strong's G25): This term means to love, emphasizing the command to love our neighbor (Mark 12:31).

Peace and Unity

- Greek: "Eirene" (εἰρήνη, Strong's G1515): This term means peace, reflecting the call to live peaceably with all (Romans 12:18).

- Greek: "Henotes" (ἑνότης, Strong's G1775): This term means unity, highlighting the importance of maintaining unity in the Spirit (Ephesians 4:3).

Comprehensive Commentary

Respecting and Valuing Diversity

The biblical concepts of honor and love are central to promoting interfaith dialogue. The Hebrew term "kabad" (Strong's H3513) and the Greek term "agapao" (Strong's G25) both emphasize the importance of respecting and valuing all people. Chaplains, by honoring the diverse religious beliefs and practices of those they serve, foster an inclusive and respectful environment.

Promoting Peace and Unity

The call to peace and unity is essential for interfaith dialogue. The Greek term "eirene" (Strong's G1515) and the Greek term "henotes" (Strong's G1775) both highlight the importance of living peaceably and maintaining unity.

Chaplains, by promoting dialogue and collaboration, contribute to a spirit of harmony and understanding.

Practical Examples of Promoting Interfaith Dialogue in Chaplaincy

In Healthcare Settings

In healthcare settings, interfaith chaplains can organize interfaith prayer services, discussion groups, and educational seminars that promote understanding and respect among patients and staff.

Proverbs 4:7 (ESV):

7. "The beginning of wisdom is this: Get wisdom, and whatever you get, get insight."

By fostering knowledge and understanding, chaplains create an inclusive and respectful environment.

In Military Settings

In military settings, interfaith chaplains can facilitate interfaith dialogue by organizing joint services, community events, and educational workshops that promote mutual respect among service members of different faiths.

James 1:19 (ESV):

19. "Know this, my beloved brothers: let every person be quick to hear, slow to speak, slow to anger."

By encouraging open and respectful dialogue, chaplains build trust and foster cooperation among service members.

In Corporate Settings

In corporate settings, interfaith chaplains can promote dialogue and cooperation by organizing interfaith discussions, cultural celebrations, and collaborative projects that address common concerns.

Ephesians 4:2-3 (ESV):

2. "With all humility and gentleness, with patience, bearing with one another in love,"

3. "eager to maintain the unity of the Spirit in the bond of peace."

By promoting dialogue and collaboration, chaplains foster a spirit of unity and respect in the workplace.

Interfaith chaplains play a crucial role in promoting dialogue and understanding between different religious communities, fostering a spirit of cooperation and mutual respect. By building bridges, reducing misunderstandings, and promoting peace, interfaith dialogue helps to create inclusive and harmonious communities. Through an exploration of biblical and theological foundations, practical strategies, and key terms, we have gained a deeper understanding of the importance and practice of promoting interfaith dialogue in chaplaincy. As we continue to navigate the challenges of interfaith ministry, the commitment to mutual respect, understanding, and inclusive care will remain central, guiding and informing the practice of chaplaincy in various settings.

CHAPTER 09

THE FUTURE OF CHAPLAINCY

Emerging Trends

Emerging trends in chaplaincy reflect the evolving needs of society and the innovative approaches chaplains are adopting to provide spiritual care. These trends include the increasing use of technology in providing spiritual care, the growing recognition of the importance of mental health, and the expanding role of chaplains in non-traditional settings. This chapter explores these trends, examining how they are shaping the future of chaplaincy and enhancing the ability of chaplains to meet the diverse needs of those they serve.

Increasing Use of Technology in Providing Spiritual Care

The use of technology is revolutionizing the way chaplains provide spiritual care, making it more accessible and efficient.

Virtual Chaplaincy

Virtual chaplaincy involves providing spiritual care through digital platforms, such as video calls, online chat, and social media. This approach has become particularly important during times of crisis, such as the COVID-19 pandemic, when face-to-face interactions are limited.

Hebrews 10:24-25 (ESV):

24. "And let us consider how to stir up one another to love and good works,"

25. "not neglecting to meet together, as is the habit of some, but encouraging one another, and all the more as you see the Day drawing near."

Virtual chaplaincy allows for continuous support and connection, even when physical meetings are not possible.

Digital Resources and Apps

Chaplains are increasingly using digital resources and apps to provide spiritual support and guidance. These tools can include prayer apps, meditation guides, online support groups, and digital libraries of religious texts.

Psalm 119:105 (ESV):

105. "Your word is a lamp to my feet and a light to my path."

Digital resources make it easier for individuals to access spiritual guidance and support whenever they need it.

Online Training and Support for Chaplains

Technology also enables chaplains to receive ongoing training and support through online courses, webinars, and virtual peer support groups. This continuous education helps chaplains stay updated on best practices and emerging trends in spiritual care.

Proverbs 1:5 (ESV):

5. "Let the wise hear and increase in learning, and the one who understands obtain guidance."

Online training and support enhance the professional development of chaplains, enabling them to provide better care.

Growing Recognition of the Importance of Mental Health

The integration of mental health and spiritual care is an emerging trend in chaplaincy, recognizing the interconnectedness of mental, emotional, and spiritual well-being.

Holistic Care

Chaplains are increasingly adopting a holistic approach to care, addressing the mental, emotional, and spiritual needs of individuals. This approach recognizes that mental health issues often have spiritual dimensions and that spiritual care can play a crucial role in mental health recovery.

3 John 1:2 (ESV):

2. "Beloved, I pray that all may go well with you and that you may be in good health, as it goes well with your soul."

Holistic care promotes overall well-being, supporting individuals in their journey toward healing and wholeness.

Collaboration with Mental Health Professionals

Chaplains are collaborating more with mental health professionals to provide integrated care. This collaboration can include co-facilitating support groups, participating in interdisciplinary care teams, and providing spiritual support alongside clinical treatment.

Ecclesiastes 4:9-10 (ESV):

9. "Two are better than one, because they have a good reward for their toil."

10. "For if they fall, one will lift up his fellow. But woe to him who is alone when he falls and has not another to lift him up!"

Collaboration enhances the quality of care and ensures that individuals receive comprehensive support.

Training in Mental Health

Chaplains are receiving more training in mental health, including topics such as trauma-informed care, crisis intervention, and recognizing signs of mental illness. This training equips chaplains to provide more effective support to individuals experiencing mental health challenges.

Proverbs 18:15 (ESV):

15. "An intelligent heart acquires knowledge, and the ear of the wise seeks knowledge."

Training in mental health enhances the competence and confidence of chaplains in addressing mental health issues.

Expanding Role of Chaplains in Non-Traditional Settings

The role of chaplains is expanding beyond traditional settings such as hospitals, the military, and prisons to include a variety of non-traditional environments.

Corporate Chaplaincy

Corporate chaplaincy involves providing spiritual care and support to employees in the workplace. Chaplains in corporate settings address issues such as work-life balance, stress, and ethical challenges, contributing to a healthier and more supportive work environment.

Colossians 3:23-24 (ESV):

23. "Whatever you do, work heartily, as for the Lord and not for men,"

24. "knowing that from the Lord you will receive the inheritance as your reward. You are serving the Lord Christ."

Corporate chaplaincy promotes employee well-being and fosters a positive workplace culture.

School and University Chaplaincy

Chaplains in educational settings provide spiritual support to students, faculty, and staff, addressing issues such as academic stress, personal development, and ethical dilemmas. They play a crucial role in promoting a supportive and inclusive educational environment.

Proverbs 22:6 (ESV):

6. "Train up a child in the way he should go; even when he is old he will not depart from it."

School and university chaplaincy support the holistic development of students and contribute to their overall well-being.

Community and Public Sector Chaplaincy

Chaplains are increasingly serving in community and public sector roles, providing spiritual care in settings such as disaster response, law enforcement, and community organizations. These chaplains support individuals and communities during times of crisis and transition, promoting resilience and recovery.

Isaiah 61:1 (ESV):

1. "The Spirit of the Lord God is upon me, because the Lord has anointed me to bring good news to the poor; he has sent me to bind up the brokenhearted, to proclaim liberty to the captives, and the opening of the prison to those who are bound."

Community and public sector chaplaincy extend the reach of spiritual care to diverse and underserved populations.

Expository Study with Exhaustive Strong's Concordance

To deepen our understanding of these emerging trends, we turn to Strong's Exhaustive Concordance to explore key Hebrew and Greek terms.

Holistic Care

- Hebrew: "Shalom" (שָׁלוֹם, Strong's H7965): This term means peace, completeness, and well-being, reflecting the holistic approach to care (Isaiah 26:3).

Collaboration

- Greek: "Synergos" (συνεργός, Strong's G4904): This term means fellow worker or collaborator, emphasizing the importance of working together (1 Corinthians 3:9).

Comprehensive Commentary

Embracing Technology in Spiritual Care

The increasing use of technology in chaplaincy reflects the need to adapt to changing times and make spiritual care more accessible. The Hebrew term "shalom" (Strong's H7965) underscores the importance of promoting well-being and peace, which technology can facilitate by providing continuous and flexible support.

Integrating Mental Health and Spiritual Care

The growing recognition of the importance of mental health highlights the interconnectedness of mental, emotional, and spiritual well-being. The Greek term "synergos" (Strong's G4904) emphasizes the value of collaboration, which is essential for providing integrated and holistic care.

Practical Examples of Emerging Trends in Chaplaincy

Virtual Chaplaincy

Chaplains can offer virtual support through video calls, online chat, and social media, providing continuous and accessible spiritual care.

Hebrews 10:24-25 (ESV):

24. "And let us consider how to stir up one another to love and good works,"

25. "not neglecting to meet together, as is the habit of some, but encouraging one another, and all the more as you see the Day drawing near."

Virtual chaplaincy allows chaplains to maintain connection and support, even when physical meetings are not possible.

Collaboration with Mental Health Professionals

Chaplains can collaborate with mental health professionals to provide integrated care, co-facilitating support groups and participating in interdisciplinary care teams.

Ecclesiastes 4:9-10 (ESV):

9. "Two are better than one, because they have a good reward for their toil."

10. "For if they fall, one will lift up his fellow. But woe to him who is alone when he falls and has not another to lift him up!"

Collaboration enhances the quality of care and ensures comprehensive support for individuals.

Expanding Chaplaincy in Non-Traditional Settings

Chaplains can serve in corporate, educational, and community settings, providing spiritual care that addresses the unique needs of these environments.

Colossians 3:23-24 (ESV):

23. "Whatever you do, work heartily, as for the Lord and not for men,"

24. "knowing that from the Lord you will receive the inheritance as your reward. You are serving the Lord Christ."

By expanding into non-traditional settings, chaplains extend the reach of spiritual care and support a broader range of individuals.

Emerging trends in chaplaincy, including the increasing use of technology, the growing recognition of the importance of mental health, and the expanding role of chaplains in non-traditional settings, are shaping the future of spiritual care. By embracing these trends, chaplains can enhance their ability to meet the diverse needs of those they serve, promoting well-being, peace, and resilience. Through an exploration of biblical and theological foundations, practical strategies, and key terms, we have gained a deeper understanding of the importance and practice of these emerging trends in chaplaincy. As we look to the future, the commitment to innovation, collaboration, and holistic care will remain central, guiding and informing the practice of chaplaincy in various settings.

Challenges and Opportunities

The future of chaplaincy presents both challenges and opportunities, including addressing the evolving needs of diverse populations, advocating for the recognition and support of chaplaincy roles, and continuing to develop professional standards and training programs. This chapter explores these challenges and opportunities, examining how chaplains can navigate the evolving landscape to provide effective and compassionate spiritual care.

Addressing the Evolving Needs of Diverse Populations

Challenge: Cultural and Religious Diversity

One of the primary challenges in chaplaincy is addressing the cultural and religious diversity of the populations served. Chaplains must be culturally competent and sensitive to the unique beliefs and practices of individuals from various backgrounds.

Proverbs 27:17 (ESV):

17. "Iron sharpens iron, and one man sharpens another."

Opportunity: Promoting Inclusivity

Chaplains have the opportunity to promote inclusivity and understanding by fostering environments where diverse beliefs and practices are respected and valued. This can enhance the quality of care and build stronger, more cohesive communities.

Galatians 3:28 (ESV):

28. "There is neither Jew nor Greek, there is neither slave nor free, there is no male and female, for you are all one in Christ Jesus."

Advocating for the Recognition and Support of Chaplaincy Roles

Challenge: Lack of Recognition

Despite the critical role chaplains play in providing spiritual and emotional support, their contributions are often under-recognized and under-supported within organizations and communities.

1 Timothy 5:18 (ESV):

18. "For the Scripture says, 'You shall not muzzle an ox when it treads out the grain,' and, 'The laborer deserves his wages.'"

Opportunity: Advocacy and Education

Chaplains can advocate for greater recognition and support by educating organizational leaders and the public about the value of chaplaincy services. This can include sharing success stories, providing evidence of positive outcomes, and engaging in public speaking and writing.

1 Peter 3:15 (ESV):

15. "But in your hearts honor Christ the Lord as holy, always being prepared to make a defense to anyone who asks

you for a reason for the hope that is in you; yet do it with gentleness and respect."

Developing Professional Standards and Training Programs

Challenge: Varied Standards

The field of chaplaincy often lacks uniform standards and training programs, leading to inconsistencies in the quality of care provided.

James 3:1 (ESV):

1. "Not many of you should become teachers, my brothers, for you know that we who teach will be judged with greater strictness."

Opportunity: Establishing Uniform Standards

There is an opportunity to develop and implement uniform professional standards and comprehensive training programs for chaplains. This can include certification processes, continuing education requirements, and specialized training in areas such as mental health and cultural competence.

2 Timothy 2:15 (ESV):

15. "Do your best to present yourself to God as one approved, a worker who has no need to be ashamed, rightly handling the word of truth."

Integrating Chaplaincy with Other Disciplines

Challenge: Fragmentation of Care

Spiritual care is often fragmented from other forms of care, leading to gaps in service and a lack of holistic support for individuals.

Ecclesiastes 4:9-10 (ESV):

9. "Two are better than one, because they have a good reward for their toil."

10. "For if they fall, one will lift up his fellow. But woe to him who is alone when he falls and has not another to lift him up!"

Opportunity: Holistic Care Models

Chaplains can work to integrate spiritual care with other disciplines, such as healthcare, mental health, and social services, to provide holistic support. Collaborative care models can enhance overall well-being and ensure that individuals receive comprehensive support.

1 Corinthians 12:12 (ESV):

12. "For just as the body is one and has many members, and all the members of the body, though many, are one body, so it is with Christ."

Embracing Technological Advancements

Challenge: Technological Barriers

While technology offers many benefits, it also presents challenges, such as accessibility issues, digital literacy, and maintaining personal connections in virtual environments.

Proverbs 3:5-6 (ESV):

5. "Trust in the Lord with all your heart, and do not lean on your own understanding."

6. "In all your ways acknowledge him, and he will make straight your paths."

Opportunity: Expanding Reach

By embracing technological advancements, chaplains can expand their reach and provide support to individuals who may not have access to traditional forms of spiritual care. This includes virtual chaplaincy services, online support groups, and digital resources.

Daniel 12:4 (ESV):

4. "But you, Daniel, shut up the words and seal the book, until the time of the end. Many shall run to and fro, and knowledge shall increase."

Fostering Resilience and Adaptability

Challenge: Rapid Changes

The rapid pace of societal and technological changes can be challenging for chaplains to keep up with, requiring continuous learning and adaptation.

Matthew 24:42 (ESV):

42. "Therefore, stay awake, for you do not know on what day your Lord is coming."

Opportunity: Lifelong Learning

Chaplains have the opportunity to foster resilience and adaptability by committing to lifelong learning and professional development. This includes staying informed about emerging trends, participating in continuing education, and remaining flexible in their approach to care.

2 Peter 3:18 (ESV):

18. "But grow in the grace and knowledge of our Lord and Savior Jesus Christ. To him be the glory both now and to the day of eternity. Amen."

Expository Study with Exhaustive Strong's Concordance

To deepen our understanding of these challenges and opportunities, we turn to Strong's Exhaustive Concordance to explore key Hebrew and Greek terms.

Recognition and Honor

- Hebrew: "Kabod" (כָּבוֹד, Strong's H3519): This term means glory or honor, emphasizing the importance of recognizing and valuing the contributions of chaplains (Psalm 29:2).

- Greek: "Time" (τιμή, Strong's G5092): This term means honor or value, highlighting the respect we should have for those who serve (Romans 13:7).

Learning and Growth

- Greek: "Matheteuo" (μαθητεύω, Strong's G3100): This term means to disciple or teach, reflecting the importance of ongoing learning and development (Matthew 28:19).

Comprehensive Commentary

Recognizing and Valuing Chaplains

The biblical concepts of honor and value are central to advocating for the recognition and support of chaplaincy roles. The Hebrew term "kabod" (Strong's H3519) and the Greek term "time" (Strong's G5092) both emphasize the importance of recognizing and valuing the contributions of chaplains. By advocating for greater recognition and support, chaplains can enhance their impact and effectiveness.

Committing to Lifelong Learning

The commitment to lifelong learning is essential for navigating the challenges and opportunities in chaplaincy. The Greek term "matheteuo" (Strong's G3100) underscores the importance of continuous learning and growth. By embracing ongoing education and professional development, chaplains can remain adaptable and resilient in an ever-changing landscape.

Practical Examples of Addressing Challenges and Opportunities in Chaplaincy

Promoting Inclusivity

Chaplains can promote inclusivity by organizing multicultural events, providing education about diverse religious practices, and fostering environments where all individuals feel valued and respected.

Galatians 3:28 (ESV):

28. "There is neither Jew nor Greek, there is neither slave nor free, there is no male and female, for you are all one in Christ Jesus."

By celebrating diversity, chaplains create inclusive and supportive communities.

Advocating for Recognition

Chaplains can advocate for recognition by sharing success stories, providing evidence of positive outcomes, and engaging in public speaking and writing to highlight the value of chaplaincy services.

1 Peter 3:15 (ESV):

15. "But in your hearts honor Christ the Lord as holy, always being prepared to make a defense to anyone who asks

you for a reason for the hope that is in you; yet do it with gentleness and respect."

By educating others about the importance of chaplaincy, chaplains can gain greater recognition and support.

Integrating Holistic Care

Chaplains can integrate holistic care by collaborating with healthcare providers, mental health professionals, and social services to provide comprehensive support that addresses the physical, emotional, and spiritual needs of individuals.

1 Corinthians 12:12 (ESV):

12. "For just as the body is one and has many members, and all the members of the body, though many, are one body, so it is with Christ."

By working together, chaplains and other professionals can provide holistic care that enhances overall well-being.

The future of chaplaincy presents both challenges and opportunities, including addressing the evolving needs of diverse populations, advocating for the recognition and support of chaplaincy roles, and continuing to develop professional standards and training programs. By navigating these challenges and embracing the opportunities, chaplains can provide effective and compassionate spiritual care that meets the diverse needs of those they serve. Through an exploration of biblical and theological foundations, practical strategies, and key terms, we have gained a deeper understanding of the importance and practice of addressing these challenges and opportunities in chaplaincy

As we look to the future, the commitment to inclusivity, recognition, holistic care, and lifelong learning will remain central, guiding and informing the practice of chaplaincy in various settings.

Vision for the Future

A vision for the future of chaplaincy includes a commitment to inclusivity, collaboration, and innovation, ensuring that chaplains remain effective and relevant in providing spiritual care and support in an ever-changing world. This chapter explores the key components of this vision, examining how chaplains can embrace these principles to enhance their ministry and meet the diverse needs of the populations they serve.

Commitment to Inclusivity

Inclusivity is fundamental to the future of chaplaincy, as chaplains serve increasingly diverse populations.

Embracing Diversity

Chaplains must embrace and celebrate diversity, recognizing the unique cultural, religious, and personal backgrounds of those they serve. This involves providing care that respects and honors these differences.

Revelation 7:9 (ESV):

9. "After this I looked, and behold, a great multitude that no one could number, from every nation, from all tribes and peoples and languages, standing before the throne and before the Lamb, clothed in white robes, with palm branches in their hands."

Promoting Equity

Chaplains should strive to promote equity, ensuring that all individuals have access to the spiritual care and support they need, regardless of their background or circumstances.

Galatians 3:28 (ESV):

28. "There is neither Jew nor Greek, there is neither slave nor free, there is no male and female, for you are all one in Christ Jesus."

By fostering an inclusive environment, chaplains can ensure that everyone feels valued and respected.

Embracing Collaboration

Collaboration is essential for enhancing the effectiveness of chaplaincy and providing comprehensive care.

Interdisciplinary Collaboration

Chaplains should work collaboratively with professionals from other disciplines, such as healthcare, mental health, and social services, to provide holistic care that addresses the physical, emotional, and spiritual needs of individuals.

Ecclesiastes 4:9-10 (ESV):

9. "Two are better than one, because they have a good reward for their toil."

10. "For if they fall, one will lift up his fellow. But woe to him who is alone when he falls and has not another to lift him up!"

Building Partnerships

Building partnerships with religious leaders, community organizations, and other stakeholders can enhance the reach and impact of chaplaincy services. These partnerships can facilitate resource sharing, joint initiatives, and community support.

Proverbs 15:22 (ESV):

22. "Without counsel plans fail, but with many advisers they succeed."

By collaborating with others, chaplains can leverage collective strengths and resources to better serve their communities.

Fostering Innovation

Innovation is crucial for adapting to the evolving needs of society and enhancing the delivery of spiritual care.

Embracing Technology

Chaplains should embrace technological advancements to expand their reach and provide flexible, accessible spiritual care. This includes utilizing virtual platforms, digital resources, and social media to connect with individuals and offer support.

Daniel 12:4 (ESV):

4. "But you, Daniel, shut up the words and seal the book, until the time of the end. Many shall run to and fro, and knowledge shall increase."

Developing New Models of Care

Innovative models of care, such as integrated care teams, community-based chaplaincy, and specialized support programs, can address specific needs and enhance the effectiveness of chaplaincy services.

Isaiah 43:19 (ESV):

19. "Behold, I am doing a new thing; now it springs forth, do you not perceive it? I will make a way in the wilderness and rivers in the desert."

By developing new approaches, chaplains can remain relevant and responsive to the changing landscape of spiritual care.

Enhancing Professional Development

Ongoing professional development is essential for maintaining high standards of care and ensuring that chaplains are well-equipped to meet the needs of those they serve.

Continuous Education

Chaplains should engage in continuous education, including advanced training, certification programs, and specialized courses, to enhance their skills and knowledge.

2 Timothy 2:15 (ESV):

15. "Do your best to present yourself to God as one approved, a worker who has no need to be ashamed, rightly handling the word of truth."

Reflective Practice

Reflective practice involves regularly reviewing and reflecting on one's work to identify areas for improvement and growth. This practice helps chaplains maintain self-awareness and improve the quality of their care.

Psalm 139:23-24 (ESV):

23. "Search me, O God, and know my heart! Try me and know my thoughts!"

24. "And see if there be any grievous way in me, and lead me in the way everlasting!"

By engaging in reflective practice, chaplains can continuously enhance their effectiveness and professionalism.

Advocacy and Public Engagement

Advocacy and public engagement are crucial for raising awareness about the value of chaplaincy and securing support for chaplaincy services.

Promoting the Role of Chaplains

Chaplains should actively promote their role and the benefits of chaplaincy services through public speaking, writing, and community engagement. This can help increase recognition and support for their work.

1 Peter 3:15 (ESV):

15. "But in your hearts honor Christ the Lord as holy, always being prepared to make a defense to anyone who asks you for a reason for the hope that is in you; yet do it with gentleness and respect."

Engaging in Policy Advocacy

Engaging in policy advocacy involves working with policymakers and organizations to influence policies and practices that support the inclusion and funding of chaplaincy services.

Proverbs 31:8-9 (ESV):

8. "Open your mouth for the mute, for the rights of all who are destitute."

9. "Open your mouth, judge righteously, defend the rights of the poor and needy."

By advocating for supportive policies, chaplains can help ensure the sustainability and growth of their services.

Expository Study with Exhaustive Strong's Concordance

To deepen our understanding of this vision, we turn to Strong's Exhaustive Concordance to explore key Hebrew and Greek terms.

Inclusivity and Unity

- Hebrew: "Yachad" (יַחַד, Strong's H3162): This term means togetherness or unity, reflecting the importance of inclusivity (Psalm 133:1).

- Greek: "Henotes" (ἑνότης, Strong's G1775): This term means unity, highlighting the goal of bringing people together (Ephesians 4:3).

Innovation and Growth

- Greek: "Kainos" (καινός, Strong's G2537): This term means new or fresh, emphasizing the importance of innovation (Isaiah 43:19).

Comprehensive Commentary

Embracing Inclusivity and Unity

The biblical concepts of togetherness and unity are central to the vision for the future of chaplaincy. The Hebrew term "yachad" (Strong's H3162) and the Greek term "henotes" (Strong's G1775) both emphasize the importance of inclusivity and unity. By fostering environments where all individuals feel valued and respected, chaplains can create stronger, more cohesive communities.

Fostering Innovation and Growth

The commitment to innovation and growth is essential for adapting to the evolving needs of society. The Greek term "kainos" (Strong's G2537) underscores the importance of embracing new approaches and ideas. By continuously seeking innovative solutions, chaplains can enhance their effectiveness and remain relevant in providing spiritual care.

Practical Examples of Implementing the Vision

Promoting Inclusivity

Chaplains can promote inclusivity by organizing multicultural events, providing education about diverse religious practices, and fostering environments where all individuals feel valued and respected.

Galatians 3:28 (ESV):

28. "There is neither Jew nor Greek, there is neither slave nor free, there is no male and female, for you are all one in Christ Jesus."

By celebrating diversity, chaplains create inclusive and supportive communities.

Embracing Technology

Chaplains can embrace technology by offering virtual support through video calls, online chat, and social media, providing continuous and accessible spiritual care.

Daniel 12:4 (ESV):

4. "But you, Daniel, shut up the words and seal the book, until the time of the end. Many shall run to and fro, and knowledge shall increase."

Virtual chaplaincy allows chaplains to maintain connection and support, even when physical meetings are not possible.

Enhancing Professional Development

Chaplains can enhance their professional development by engaging in continuous education, participating in certification programs, and practicing reflective review.

2 Timothy 2:15 (ESV):

15. "Do your best to present yourself to God as one approved, a worker who has no need to be ashamed, rightly handling the word of truth."

By committing to lifelong learning, chaplains can maintain high standards of care and remain effective in their ministry.

A vision for the future of chaplaincy includes a commitment to inclusivity, collaboration, and innovation, ensuring that chaplains remain effective and relevant in providing spiritual care and support in an ever-changing world. By embracing these principles, chaplains can enhance their ministry, meet the diverse needs of the populations they serve, and contribute to the well-being and cohesion of their communities. Through an exploration of biblical and theological foundations, practical strategies, and key terms, we have gained a deeper understanding of this vision for the future. As we move forward, the commitment to inclusivity, collaboration, and innovation will guide and inform the practice of chaplaincy, ensuring that it continues to thrive and make a meaningful impact in the lives of individuals and communities.

CONCLUSION

SUMMARY OF KEY POINTS

Summary of Key Points

This book has explored the theological foundations of chaplaincy, providing a comprehensive understanding of its role, challenges, and significance. By examining the historical development, core theological principles, and practical aspects of chaplaincy, we have gained valuable insights into the unique ministry of chaplains. This concluding chapter summarizes the key points covered in each chapter, highlighting the essential themes and insights that have emerged throughout this exploration.

Chapter 1: Introduction

We began with an introduction to chaplaincy, defining it as a unique ministry that provides spiritual care and support in various secular settings, such as the military, hospitals, prisons, universities, and workplaces. Unlike traditional parish ministry, chaplains work within organizations that may not have a specific religious affiliation, serving individuals from diverse backgrounds and beliefs. The purpose of the book was established: to explore the theological foundations of chaplaincy and provide a comprehensive understanding of its role, challenges, and significance in contemporary society.

Chapter 2: Historical Overview of Chaplaincy

The historical development of chaplaincy was traced from its early beginnings to the present day. We explored the origins of chaplaincy in the early Christian church, where clergy provided spiritual care to soldiers and prisoners. Key milestones included the establishment of military chaplaincy during the Crusades, the rise of hospital chaplaincy in medieval Europe, and the formal recognition of prison chaplaincy in the 19th century. The modern era has seen chaplaincy become an integral part of many institutions, with professional standards and training programs developed to ensure the effectiveness and ethical conduct of chaplains.

Chapter 3: Theological Foundations of Chaplaincy

The theological foundations of chaplaincy were examined, emphasizing the biblical basis for chaplaincy, the ministry of presence, serving the marginalized, the concept of incarnation, compassion, and reconciliation. Key scriptural themes included the ministry of presence (Psalm 23), the call to serve the marginalized (Luke 4:18-19), and the model of Jesus as the ultimate shepherd and healer (John 10:14). The chapter underscored the importance of chaplains embodying these theological principles in their ministry.

Chapter 4: The Role of the Chaplain

The diverse roles and responsibilities of chaplains were outlined, including providing spiritual care, offering counseling and support, leading religious services, and advocating for the needs of those they serve. Core responsibilities such as spiritual care, counseling, and support were discussed in detail, emphasizing the chaplain's role in addressing the holistic needs of individuals. The skills and qualities essential for effective chaplaincy, such as empathy, active listening, cultural competence, and ethical integrity, were also highlighted.

Chapter 5: Chaplaincy in Different Contexts

The various contexts in which chaplains serve were explored, including military chaplaincy, hospital chaplaincy, prison chaplaincy, university chaplaincy, and workplace chaplaincy. Each context presents unique challenges and opportunities for chaplains, requiring them to adapt their approach to meet the specific needs of the individuals and communities they serve. Practical examples of chaplaincy in these settings illustrated the diverse applications of chaplaincy and the impact of chaplains on those they serve.

Chapter 6: Pastoral Care and Counseling

The nature of pastoral care and counseling was examined, highlighting the holistic approach chaplains take to address the spiritual, emotional, and relational needs of individuals. Counseling techniques such as cognitive-behavioral therapy, solution-focused therapy, narrative therapy, and crisis intervention were discussed in detail, providing insights into how chaplains support individuals through various challenges. The importance of maintaining confidentiality and establishing appropriate boundaries in pastoral care was also emphasized.

Chapter 7: Ethical Challenges in Chaplaincy

Ethical challenges in chaplaincy were addressed, focusing on the importance of maintaining confidentiality, establishing and maintaining appropriate boundaries, and practicing cultural competence. The chapter discussed the need for chaplains to navigate these challenges with sensitivity and integrity, ensuring that their care is ethical and respectful of the diverse backgrounds and beliefs of those they serve. Practical strategies for managing confidentiality, boundaries, and cultural competence were provided.

Chapter 8: Interfaith Chaplaincy

The role of interfaith chaplains in promoting dialogue and understanding between different religious communities was explored. The chapter emphasized the importance of navigating religious diversity with sensitivity and respect, recognizing the unique beliefs and practices of different faith traditions. Practical strategies for promoting interfaith dialogue, such as facilitating interfaith events, encouraging open and respectful dialogue, and building relationships with religious leaders, were discussed.

Chapter 9: The Future of Chaplaincy

The future of chaplaincy was examined, highlighting emerging trends, challenges, and opportunities. Key trends included the increasing use of technology in providing spiritual care, the growing recognition of the importance of mental health, and the expanding role of chaplains in non-traditional settings. The chapter also outlined a vision for the future of chaplaincy, emphasizing a commitment to inclusivity, collaboration, and innovation. The importance of continuous professional development, advocacy, and public engagement in shaping the future of chaplaincy was underscored.

Throughout this book, we have explored the theological foundations of chaplaincy, providing a comprehensive understanding of its role, challenges, and significance. We have traced the historical development of chaplaincy, examined its core theological principles, and explored its practical applications in various contexts. By addressing the ethical challenges and emerging trends in chaplaincy, we have gained valuable insights into the future of this unique ministry.

As we look to the future, the commitment to inclusivity, collaboration, and innovation will remain central, guiding and informing the practice of chaplaincy in various settings. Chaplains will continue to play a vital role in providing spiritual care and support, fostering understanding and respect, and promoting the well-being of individuals and communities. This book serves as a resource and guide for current and aspiring chaplains, theologians, and anyone interested in the intersection of faith and service, offering a deeper understanding of the unique and essential ministry of chaplaincy.

FINAL REFLECTIONS

Chaplaincy is a vital and dynamic ministry that embodies the love and compassion of God in diverse and often challenging settings. As chaplains continue to adapt and evolve, their commitment to providing holistic spiritual care remains unwavering, reflecting the heart of God's mission in the world. This chapter offers final reflections on the significance of chaplaincy, the enduring qualities of effective chaplains, and the hopeful future of this essential ministry.

The Significance of Chaplaincy

Chaplaincy holds a unique place in the landscape of spiritual care, providing support in environments that are often secular and complex. Chaplains serve in hospitals, prisons, military units, universities, workplaces, and many other settings where traditional religious support might not be readily available. They meet people where they are, offering comfort, guidance, and hope in times of crisis, transition, and daily life.

Matthew 25:35-36 (ESV):

35. "For I was hungry and you gave me food, I was thirsty and you gave me drink, I was a stranger and you welcomed me,"

36. "I was naked and you clothed me, I was sick and you visited me, I was in prison and you came to me."

This scripture encapsulates the essence of chaplaincy: a ministry of presence, care, and compassion that addresses the physical, emotional, and spiritual needs of individuals.

The Enduring Qualities of Effective Chaplains

Effective chaplains embody several enduring qualities that enable them to fulfill their ministry with integrity and grace:

Compassion and Empathy

Chaplains must be deeply compassionate, able to empathize with those they serve and offer genuine care and support.

Colossians 3:12 (ESV):

12. "Put on then, as God's chosen ones, holy and beloved, compassionate hearts, kindness, humility, meekness, and patience."

Cultural Competence and Inclusivity

Chaplains must be culturally competent, respecting and valuing the diverse backgrounds and beliefs of those they serve. This inclusivity fosters trust and creates a welcoming environment for all individuals.

Galatians 3:28 (ESV):

28. "There is neither Jew nor Greek, there is neither slave nor free, there is no male and female, for you are all one in Christ Jesus."

Adaptability and Innovation

The ability to adapt and innovate is crucial for chaplains as they navigate changing environments and emerging challenges. Embracing new technologies and approaches enhances their capacity to provide effective care.

Isaiah 43:19 (ESV):

19. "Behold, I am doing a new thing; now it springs forth, do you not perceive it? I will make a way in the wilderness and rivers in the desert."

Commitment to Lifelong Learning

Continuous learning and professional development are essential for chaplains to stay informed and skilled in their ministry. This commitment ensures that they can offer the highest quality of care.

Proverbs 1:5 (ESV):

5. "Let the wise hear and increase in learning, and the one who understands obtain guidance."

The Hopeful Future of Chaplaincy

The future of chaplaincy is filled with promise and potential. As society continues to evolve, the role of chaplains will remain crucial in addressing the spiritual and emotional needs of diverse populations. By embracing inclusivity, collaboration, and innovation, chaplains can continue to expand their impact and reach.

Expanding Reach through Technology

The integration of technology in chaplaincy practices allows chaplains to reach more people, offering virtual support and digital resources that make spiritual care more accessible.

Psalm 119:105 (ESV):

105. "Your word is a lamp to my feet and a light to my path."

Strengthening Collaboration

Building stronger partnerships with healthcare providers, mental health professionals, and community organizations can enhance the holistic care chaplains provide, addressing the comprehensive needs of individuals.

1 Corinthians 12:12 (ESV):

12. "For just as the body is one and has many members, and all the members of the body, though many, are one body, so it is with Christ."

Advocating for Recognition and Support

Chaplains can advocate for greater recognition and support for their roles, highlighting the critical value they bring to various settings. This advocacy can lead to increased resources and opportunities for chaplaincy services.

Proverbs 31:8-9 (ESV):

8. "Open your mouth for the mute, for the rights of all who are destitute."

9. "Open your mouth, judge righteously, defend the rights of the poor and needy."

Chaplaincy is a ministry that profoundly embodies the love and compassion of God, offering holistic spiritual care in diverse and often challenging settings. As chaplains continue to adapt and evolve, their commitment to this sacred calling remains steadfast. By embracing inclusivity, fostering collaboration, and driving innovation, chaplains can continue to reflect the heart of God's mission in the world.

This book has provided a comprehensive exploration of the theological foundations, historical development, practical aspects, and future directions of chaplaincy. Through this journey, we have gained valuable insights into the unique and essential ministry of chaplains, who serve as beacons of hope, comfort, and spiritual guidance.

As we look to the future, the dedication and resilience of chaplains will ensure that they continue to make a meaningful impact in the lives of individuals and communities, reflecting the enduring presence of God's love and compassion in the world.

APPENDIX A

SAMPLE CHAPLAINCY POLICIES AND PROCEDURES

This appendix provides sample policies and procedures for chaplaincy services in various settings. These policies and procedures are designed to ensure the effective and ethical provision of spiritual care, addressing key aspects such as confidentiality, boundaries, cultural competence, and professional development. While these samples can serve as a guide, it is important for organizations to tailor their policies and procedures to meet their specific needs and contexts.

Policy on Confidentiality

Purpose

To ensure that all chaplaincy interactions are conducted with the utmost respect for the privacy and confidentiality of individuals served.

Policy

1. Confidentiality Commitment: Chaplains must maintain confidentiality in all interactions, respecting the privacy of individuals and the sensitive nature of the information shared.

2. Exceptions: Confidentiality may be breached only under the following circumstances:

- If the individual poses a danger to themselves or others.

- If there is a legal obligation to disclose information (e.g., mandatory reporting of abuse).

3. Record Keeping: Any records kept by chaplains must be stored securely and accessed only by authorized personnel. Electronic records should be password-protected and encrypted.

Procedures

1. Informing Individuals: At the beginning of any interaction, chaplains should inform individuals about the confidentiality policy and the exceptions.

2. Documentation: Chaplains should document any breaches of confidentiality, including the reason for the breach and the steps taken.

3. Training: Chaplains will receive regular training on confidentiality policies and procedures.

Policy on Boundaries

Purpose

To establish clear boundaries that ensure professional and ethical relationships between chaplains and those they serve.

Policy

1. Professional Boundaries: Chaplains must maintain professional boundaries at all times, avoiding relationships that could impair their professional judgment or lead to conflicts of interest.

2. Personal Involvement: Chaplains should avoid becoming overly involved in the personal lives of those they serve, maintaining a professional distance.

3. Dual Relationships: Chaplains should avoid dual relationships that could compromise their objectivity or create a conflict of interest.

Procedures

1. Boundary Training: Chaplains will receive training on maintaining professional boundaries and identifying potential boundary issues.

2. Supervision and Support: Regular supervision and peer support sessions will be provided to help chaplains navigate boundary issues.

3. Reporting Concerns: Chaplains should report any boundary concerns to their supervisor immediately.

Policy on Cultural Competence

Purpose

To ensure that chaplains provide culturally competent care that respects the diverse backgrounds and beliefs of individuals served.

Policy

1. Respect for Diversity: Chaplains must respect and value the cultural, religious, and personal backgrounds of all individuals.

2. Ongoing Education: Chaplains are required to engage in ongoing education to enhance their cultural competence.

3. Inclusive Practices: Chaplains should use inclusive language and practices that honor the diverse beliefs and practices of those they serve.

Procedures

1. Cultural Competence Training: Regular training sessions will be provided to enhance chaplains' understanding of cultural competence.

2. Resource Utilization: Chaplains should utilize cultural competence resources, such as cultural guides and community liaisons, to better understand and serve diverse populations.

3. Feedback Mechanism: A feedback mechanism will be established to allow individuals to share their experiences and suggest improvements in cultural competence practices.

Policy on Professional Development

Purpose

To ensure that chaplains engage in continuous professional development to maintain high standards of care.

Policy

1. Continuous Learning: Chaplains must engage in continuous professional development, including attending workshops, conferences, and training programs.

2. Certification and Licensure: Chaplains are encouraged to obtain and maintain relevant certifications and licensure.

3. Reflective Practice: Chaplains should engage in regular reflective practice to evaluate and improve their care.

Procedures

1. Professional Development Plan: Each chaplain will develop a professional development plan in consultation with their supervisor.

2. Training Opportunities: The organization will provide access to training opportunities, including workshops, online courses, and conferences.

3. Evaluation and Feedback: Regular evaluations will be conducted to assess chaplains' professional development progress and provide constructive feedback.

Policy on Ethical Conduct

Purpose

To ensure that chaplains adhere to high ethical standards in all aspects of their ministry.

Policy

1. Code of Ethics: Chaplains must adhere to the organization's code of ethics, which outlines the principles of ethical conduct.

2. Conflict of Interest: Chaplains must disclose any potential conflicts of interest and avoid situations that could compromise their ethical judgment.

3. Accountability: Chaplains are accountable for their actions and must report any ethical concerns to their supervisor.

Procedures

1. Ethics Training: Regular ethics training will be provided to ensure that chaplains understand and adhere to the code of ethics.

2. Ethical Decision-Making: Chaplains will receive training in ethical decision-making to help navigate complex ethical dilemmas.

3. Reporting Mechanism: A reporting mechanism will be established for chaplains to report ethical concerns confidentially.

Policy on Crisis Intervention

Purpose

To provide guidelines for chaplains in responding to crises, ensuring effective and compassionate care.

Policy

1. Crisis Response: Chaplains must be prepared to respond to crises, providing immediate support and stabilization.

2. Training and Preparedness: Chaplains will receive training in crisis intervention techniques and preparedness.

3. Collaboration: Chaplains should collaborate with other professionals and organizations to provide comprehensive crisis support.

Procedures

1. Crisis Intervention Training: Chaplains will receive regular training in crisis intervention techniques, including psychological first aid and de-escalation strategies.

2. Crisis Response Plan: A crisis response plan will be developed and regularly updated to guide chaplains in responding to various types of crises.

3. Debriefing and Support: After a crisis intervention, chaplains will participate in debriefing sessions to process the experience and receive support.

These sample policies and procedures provide a framework for effective and ethical chaplaincy practice. Organizations should adapt and expand upon these samples to meet their specific needs and contexts, ensuring that chaplains are well-equipped to provide compassionate and competent spiritual care. By adhering to these guidelines, chaplains can uphold the highest standards of professionalism and integrity in their ministry.

CHAPLAINCY TRAINING PROGRAMS AND RESOURCES

This appendix provides an overview of various training programs and resources available to chaplains. These programs and resources are designed to enhance the skills, knowledge, and competencies of chaplains, ensuring they can provide effective and compassionate spiritual care. While this list is not exhaustive, it highlights key programs and resources that can support chaplains in their professional development.

Chaplaincy Training Programs

Clinical Pastoral Education (CPE)

Overview: Clinical Pastoral Education (CPE) is a structured, experiential education program that provides training in pastoral care. CPE programs are typically offered in healthcare settings, such as hospitals and hospices, and include supervised clinical practice, peer group learning, and individual reflection.

Accreditation: Many CPE programs are accredited by organizations such as the Association for Clinical Pastoral Education (ACPE) in the United States or the College of Pastoral Supervision and Psychotherapy (CPSP).

Key Components:

- Supervised clinical practice

- Peer group learning

- Individual reflection and supervision

- Development of pastoral identity and skills

Website: [ACPE](https://www.acpe.edu) | [CPSP](https://www.cpsp.org)

Military Chaplaincy Training

Overview: Military chaplaincy training programs are designed to prepare chaplains for service in the armed forces. These programs typically include basic officer training, specialized chaplaincy training, and ongoing professional development.

Accreditation: Training is typically provided by the respective military branches, such as the U.S. Army Chaplain Center and School or the Royal Canadian Chaplain Service.

Key Components:

- Basic officer training

- Specialized chaplaincy training

- Field exercises and simulations

- Ongoing professional development and continuing education

Website: [U.S. Army Chaplain Corps](https://www.goarmy.com/careers-and-jobs/specialty-careers/chaplain.html) | [Royal Canadian Chaplain Service](https://www.canada.ca/en/department-national-defence/services/benefits-military/chaplain.html)

Hospital Chaplaincy Training

Overview: Hospital chaplaincy training programs focus on providing spiritual care in healthcare settings. These programs often include CPE components, specialized courses in medical ethics, and training in palliative and end-of-life care.

Accreditation: Programs may be offered through hospitals, healthcare organizations, and academic institutions, often in collaboration with accrediting bodies such as ACPE.

Key Components:

- Clinical practice in healthcare settings

- Training in medical ethics and healthcare systems

- Specialized courses in palliative and end-of-life care

- Supervision and reflective practice

Website: [Association of Professional Chaplains](https://www.professionalchaplains.org)

Prison Chaplaincy Training

Overview: Prison chaplaincy training programs prepare chaplains to provide spiritual care and support to incarcerated individuals. These programs include training in correctional systems, restorative justice, and crisis intervention.

Accreditation: Training is often provided by correctional institutions, faith-based organizations, and academic institutions.

Key Components:

- Understanding of correctional systems

- Training in restorative justice and rehabilitation

- Crisis intervention and conflict resolution skills

- Ethical considerations in prison chaplaincy

Website: [American Correctional Chaplains Association](https://www.correctionalchaplains.org)

University Chaplaincy Training

Overview: University chaplaincy training programs focus on providing spiritual care and support in academic settings. These programs often include training in counseling, student development, and interfaith dialogue.

Accreditation: Programs may be offered through academic institutions, religious organizations, and professional chaplaincy associations.

Key Components:

- Counseling and support for students, faculty, and staff

- Understanding of student development theories

- Training in interfaith dialogue and cultural competence

- Program development and leadership skills

Website: [Association of College and University Religious Affairs](https://www.acura.org)

Online Training and Continuing Education

Online Chaplaincy Courses

Overview: Various organizations and institutions offer online chaplaincy courses that provide flexible and accessible training opportunities for chaplains. These courses cover a wide range of topics, including pastoral care, ethics, and specialized areas of chaplaincy.

Key Components:

- Flexible, self-paced learning

- Wide range of topics and specializations

- Access to expert instructors and resources

Website: [Chaplaincy Institute](https://chaplaincyinstitute.org) | [Spiritual Care Association](https://www.spiritualcareassociation.org)

Webinars and Workshops

Overview: Webinars and workshops provide opportunities for chaplains to engage in professional development on specific topics. These events are often hosted by professional chaplaincy organizations and can be attended live or accessed as recordings.

Key Components:

- Interactive learning experiences

- Focus on specific topics and skills

- Networking opportunities with other chaplains

Website: [Association of Professional Chaplains](https://www.professionalchaplains.org) | [National Association of Catholic Chaplains](https://www.nacc.org)

Certification Programs

Overview: Certification programs provide formal recognition of a chaplain's skills and competencies. These programs often include coursework, supervised practice, and examinations.

Key Components:

- Comprehensive training and assessment

- Formal certification and recognition

- Ongoing professional development requirements

Website: [Board of Chaplaincy Certification Inc.](https://bcci.professionalchaplains.org) | [National Association of Catholic Chaplains](https://www.nacc.org)

Professional Organizations and Resources

Professional Chaplaincy Associations

Overview: Professional chaplaincy associations provide resources, networking opportunities, and support for chaplains. Membership in these associations often includes access to conferences, publications, and continuing education opportunities.

Key Associations:

- [Association of Professional Chaplains](https://www.professionalchaplains.org)

- [National Association of Catholic Chaplains](https://www.nacc.org)

- [Spiritual Care Association](https://www.spiritualcareassociation.org)

Publications and Journals

Overview: Publications and journals offer valuable insights, research, and best practices in chaplaincy. Subscribing to these resources can help chaplains stay informed about the latest developments in the field.

Key Publications:

- Journal of Pastoral Care & Counseling

- Chaplaincy Today

- Journal of Health Care Chaplaincy

Online Resources and Libraries

Overview: Online resources and libraries provide access to a wealth of information, including articles, research papers, and practical tools for chaplains.

Key Resources:

- [The Chaplaincy Innovation Lab](https://chaplaincyinnovation.org)

- [The National Association of Catholic Chaplains Resource Library](https://www.nacc.org/resources)

This appendix has provided an overview of various training programs and resources available to chaplains. These programs and resources are designed to enhance the skills, knowledge, and competencies of chaplains, ensuring they can provide effective and compassionate spiritual care. By engaging in these opportunities, chaplains can continue to grow professionally and remain well-equipped to meet the diverse needs of those they serve.

APPENDIX C

CASE STUDIES IN CHAPLAINCY

Case studies provide valuable insights into the practical application of chaplaincy principles and the impact of chaplaincy services in various settings. This appendix presents several case studies that illustrate the challenges, strategies, and outcomes of chaplaincy interventions. These case studies highlight the diverse roles chaplains play and the significant difference they make in the lives of individuals and communities.

Case Study 1: Hospital Chaplaincy - Providing Comfort in Crisis

Background

John, a 65-year-old man, was admitted to the hospital with severe pneumonia. His condition rapidly deteriorated, and he was placed in the Intensive Care Unit (ICU). John's family, deeply religious and close-knit, was devastated and in need of spiritual support.

Intervention

The hospital chaplain, Sarah, received a referral from the ICU staff to provide support to John's family. She introduced herself to the family, offering a compassionate presence and listening to their concerns and fears. Sarah provided spiritual counsel, prayed with the family, and facilitated a bedside prayer vigil.

Outcome

Sarah's presence and support helped the family feel less isolated and more hopeful. She coordinated with the medical team to ensure the family's spiritual needs were considered in John's care plan. When John passed away, Sarah continued to support the family through their grief, offering comfort and resources for bereavement support. The family expressed deep gratitude for Sarah's care, which they felt honored John's faith and brought them solace during a difficult time.

Reflection

This case study illustrates the critical role of hospital chaplains in providing comfort and spiritual support during medical crises. By offering a compassionate presence and addressing the spiritual needs of patients and families, chaplains help mitigate the emotional and spiritual distress associated with illness and loss.

Case Study 2: Military Chaplaincy - Building Resilience

Background

Captain Mark, a military chaplain, was deployed with his unit to a conflict zone. The soldiers in his unit faced daily stress and danger, leading to high levels of anxiety and emotional strain. Several soldiers struggled with maintaining their mental health and resilience.

Intervention

Mark implemented a comprehensive chaplaincy program focused on building resilience and providing emotional and spiritual support. He conducted regular stress management workshops, facilitated peer support groups, and offered one-on-one counseling sessions. Mark also organized interfaith prayer services and created a safe space for soldiers to discuss their fears and concerns.

Outcome

The soldiers reported feeling more supported and better equipped to handle the stresses of deployment. Mark's efforts contributed to improved morale and cohesion within the unit. His program also helped identify soldiers in need of additional mental health support, ensuring they received timely and appropriate care.

Reflection

This case study highlights the importance of military chaplains in promoting resilience and mental well-being among service members. Through targeted interventions and holistic support, chaplains play a vital role in enhancing the overall health and readiness of military personnel.

Case Study 3: Prison Chaplaincy - Facilitating Transformation

Background

David, a 30-year-old inmate serving a long-term sentence, struggled with feelings of hopelessness and anger. He had a history of conflict with other inmates and staff and showed little interest in rehabilitation programs.

Intervention

The prison chaplain, Rachel, reached out to David and began regular pastoral visits. She built a rapport with him, listening to his story without judgment and offering spiritual guidance. Rachel encouraged David to join a restorative justice program and facilitated his participation in a prison-based faith group.

Outcome

Over time, David's attitude began to change. He became actively involved in the faith group, finding a sense of purpose and community. The restorative justice program helped him address his past actions and work towards reconciliation. David's behavior improved, and he started mentoring other inmates, sharing his journey of transformation.

Reflection

This case study demonstrates the transformative potential of prison chaplaincy. By providing consistent spiritual support and facilitating programs that promote healing and growth, chaplains can help inmates find meaning and direction, leading to positive changes in behavior and outlook.

Case Study 4: University Chaplaincy - Supporting Mental Health

Background

Emily, a sophomore at a large university, began experiencing severe anxiety and depression due to academic pressures and personal issues. She felt overwhelmed and isolated, struggling to find balance and support.

Intervention

The university chaplain, James, was alerted to Emily's situation by a concerned professor. James reached out to Emily, offering a confidential and supportive space to discuss her struggles. He provided spiritual counseling and connected her with mental health resources on campus. James also invited Emily to join a student support group he facilitated.

Outcome

Emily found relief in sharing her experiences with James and the support group. She began to implement coping strategies and accessed mental health services for ongoing support. Her academic performance and overall well-being improved, and she expressed gratitude for the chaplaincy support that helped her navigate a difficult period.

Reflection

This case study highlights the crucial role of university chaplains in supporting student mental health. By providing compassionate care, connecting students to resources, and fostering supportive communities, chaplains help students manage stress and thrive in their academic and personal lives.

Case Study 5: Workplace Chaplaincy - Enhancing Employee Well-being

Background

A large corporation experienced a series of layoffs, leading to increased stress and uncertainty among remaining employees. Productivity and morale were significantly affected, and management sought ways to support their workforce.

Intervention

The company's chaplain, Linda, initiated a comprehensive employee support program. She offered individual counseling sessions, facilitated stress management workshops, and organized team-building activities. Linda also provided spiritual care for employees seeking guidance and facilitated discussions on coping with change and loss.

Outcome

Employees reported feeling more supported and valued through Linda's initiatives. The workshops and counseling sessions helped reduce stress levels and improve morale. Management noticed an improvement in productivity and employee engagement, attributing it to the chaplaincy support provided during a challenging time.

Reflection

This case study illustrates the positive impact of workplace chaplaincy on employee well-being and organizational health. By addressing the emotional and spiritual needs of employees, chaplains help create a more supportive and resilient work environment.

Conclusion

These case studies demonstrate the diverse roles and significant impact of chaplains in various settings. From providing comfort in hospitals and building resilience in the military to facilitating transformation in prisons, supporting mental health in universities, and enhancing well-being in workplaces, chaplains play a vital role in addressing the spiritual and emotional needs of individuals and communities. Through their compassionate presence and holistic approach to care, chaplains embody the love and compassion of God, making a meaningful difference in the lives of those they serve.

REFERENCES

This section provides a list of books, articles, and other resources on the theology and practice of chaplaincy. These references are valuable for anyone interested in deepening their understanding of chaplaincy, its theological foundations, and practical applications.

Books

1. Holst, Lawrence E. (2006). Hospital Ministry: The Role of the Chaplain Today. Wipf & Stock Publishers.

   - This book provides an in-depth look at the role of hospital chaplains and the unique challenges and opportunities they face in providing spiritual care in healthcare settings.

2. Miller-McLemore, Bonnie J. (2012). The Wiley-Blackwell Companion to Practical Theology. Wiley-Blackwell.

   - A comprehensive resource that covers various aspects of practical theology, including chapters on chaplaincy and pastoral care.

3. Paget, Naomi K., & McCormack, Janet R. (2006). The Work of the Chaplain. Judson Press.

- This book explores the diverse roles of chaplains in different settings, providing practical guidance and insights into the chaplaincy profession.

4. Nolan, Steve. (2011). Spiritual Care at the End of Life: The Chaplain as a "Hopeful Presence". Jessica Kingsley Publishers.

- Focuses on the role of chaplains in providing spiritual care at the end of life, emphasizing the importance of hope and presence.

5. Lartey, Emmanuel Y. (2003). In Living Color: An Intercultural Approach to Pastoral Care and Counseling. Jessica Kingsley Publishers.

- Examines pastoral care and counseling from an intercultural perspective, offering valuable insights for chaplains working in diverse settings.

6. Vande Creek, Larry, & Burton, Arthur M. (2001). Professional Chaplaincy: What Is Happening to It?. Haworth Press.

- Discusses the evolving role of professional chaplaincy and the challenges and opportunities facing chaplains today.

Articles

1. Cadge, Wendy. (2012). "Paging God: Religion in the Halls of Medicine". The University of Chicago Press.

- An article exploring the presence and role of religion and chaplaincy in medical settings, based on extensive research and interviews.

2. Fitchett, George, et al. (2015). "Evidence-Based Chaplaincy Care: Attitudes and Practices in Diverse Healthcare Chaplain Samples". Journal of Health Care Chaplaincy, 21(2), 55-75.

- This study investigates the attitudes and practices of healthcare chaplains regarding evidence-based care, highlighting the importance of research and best practices in chaplaincy.

3. Pargament, Kenneth I. (2007). "Spiritually Integrated Psychotherapy: Understanding and Addressing the Sacred". Guilford Press.

An article discussing the integration of spirituality into psychotherapy, providing valuable insights for chaplains involved in counseling and mental health support.

4. Tisdale, Theresa A. (2003). "Listening to Theological Voices in Pastoral Counseling". Journal of Psychology and Theology, 31(2), 139-151.

- Explores the role of theological perspectives in pastoral counseling, offering guidance for chaplains in integrating theology into their practice.

5. Koenig, Harold G. (2012). "Religion, Spirituality, and Health: The Research and Clinical Implications". ISRN Psychiatry, 2012, Article ID 278730.

- Reviews research on the relationship between religion, spirituality, and health, and discusses the implications for clinical practice, including chaplaincy.

Online Resources

1. Association of Professional Chaplains: https://www.professionalchaplains.org

- Provides resources, certification information, and continuing education opportunities for professional chaplains.

2. Spiritual Care Association: https://www.spiritualcareassociation.org

- Offers training, resources, and support for chaplains and spiritual care providers.

3. Chaplaincy Innovation Lab: https://chaplaincyinnovation.org

- A platform for sharing research, resources, and best practices in chaplaincy across various settings.

4. Journal of Health Care Chaplaincy: https://www.tandfonline.com/toc/whcc20/current

- A peer-reviewed journal featuring research articles, reviews, and practical insights relevant to healthcare chaplaincy.

5. The National Association of Catholic Chaplains: https://www.nacc.org

- Provides resources, certification programs, and support for Catholic chaplains and those involved in spiritual care.

These books, articles, and online resources offer a wealth of knowledge and insights into the theology and practice of chaplaincy. Whether you are a current chaplain, an aspiring chaplain, or simply interested in the field, these references provide valuable information to enhance your understanding and practice of chaplaincy. By engaging with these resources, you can deepen your knowledge, develop your skills, and continue to grow in your ministry.

SCRIPTURAL REFERENCES AND THEOLOGICAL TEXTS

Scriptural References and Theological Texts Relevant to the Themes Discussed in the Book

This appendix provides a compilation of scriptural references and theological texts that are relevant to the themes discussed throughout the book. These references serve as foundational texts that inform the practice of chaplaincy and its theological underpinnings.

Scriptural References

Ministry of Presence

Psalm 23:4 (ESV):

4. "Even though I walk through the valley of the shadow of death, I will fear no evil, for you are with me; your rod and your staff, they comfort me."

Serving the Marginalized

Luke 4:18-19 (ESV):

18. "The Spirit of the Lord is upon me, because he has anointed me to proclaim good news to the poor. He has sent me to proclaim liberty to the captives and recovering of sight to the blind, to set at liberty those who are oppressed,"

19. "to proclaim the year of the Lord's favor."

Incarnation

John 1:14 (ESV):

14. "And the Word became flesh and dwelt among us, and we have seen his glory, glory as of the only Son from the Father, full of grace and truth."

Compassion

Matthew 9:36 (ESV):

36. "When he saw the crowds, he had compassion for them, because they were harassed and helpless, like sheep without a shepherd."

Reconciliation

2 Corinthians 5:18-19 (ESV):

18. "All this is from God, who through Christ reconciled us to himself and gave us the ministry of reconciliation;"

19. "that is, in Christ God was reconciling the world to himself, not counting their trespasses against them, and entrusting to us the message of reconciliation."

Inclusivity

Galatians 3:28 (ESV):

28. "There is neither Jew nor Greek, there is neither slave nor free, there is no male and female, for you are all one in Christ Jesus."

Unity and Collaboration

Ephesians 4:2-3 (ESV):

2. "With all humility and gentleness, with patience, bearing with one another in love,"

3. "eager to maintain the unity of the Spirit in the bond of peace."

Ethical Conduct

1 Timothy 5:18 (ESV):

18. "For the Scripture says, 'You shall not muzzle an ox when it treads out the grain,' and, 'The laborer deserves his wages.'"

Lifelong Learning

Proverbs 1:5 (ESV):

5. "Let the wise hear and increase in learning, and the one who understands obtain guidance."

Theological Texts

On Pastoral Care and Counseling

Clinebell, Howard. (2011). Basic Types of Pastoral Care and Counseling: Resources for the Ministry of Healing and Growth. Abingdon Press.

- A foundational text that provides a comprehensive guide to pastoral care and counseling, offering practical approaches and theological insights.

On Spiritual Care in Healthcare

Koenig, Harold G. (2002). Spirituality in Patient Care: Why, How, When, and What. Templeton Foundation Press.

- This book explores the integration of spirituality into patient care, providing guidelines and research-based practices for healthcare chaplains.

On Interfaith Chaplaincy

Cornille, Catherine. (2013). The Im-Possibility of Interreligious Dialogue. Crossroad Publishing.

- An insightful text that addresses the challenges and possibilities of interfaith dialogue, offering valuable perspectives for interfaith chaplains.

On Theological Foundations of Chaplaincy

Pattison, Stephen. (2000). A Critique of Pastoral Care. SCM Press.

- A critical examination of the assumptions and practices of pastoral care, providing a robust theological foundation for chaplaincy.

On Compassion and Presence

Nouwen, Henri J.M. (1986). The Wounded Healer: Ministry in Contemporary Society. Image Books.

- A classic text that explores the role of the minister as a compassionate presence, drawing on the author's experiences and insights.

On Ethics and Professionalism

Trull, Joe E., & Carter, R. Robert. (2004). Ministerial Ethics: Moral Formation for Church Leaders. Baker Academic.

- A comprehensive guide to ethical issues in ministry, offering practical guidance for maintaining integrity and professionalism in chaplaincy.

On Inclusivity and Cultural Competence

Lartey, Emmanuel Y. (2003). In Living Color: An Intercultural Approach to Pastoral Care and Counseling. Jessica Kingsley Publishers.

- This book examines pastoral care from an intercultural perspective, providing valuable insights for chaplains working in diverse settings.

The scriptural references and theological texts listed in this appendix provide a robust foundation for the themes discussed throughout the book. These resources offer valuable insights and guidance for chaplains as they navigate the complexities of their ministry, providing compassionate and effective spiritual care. By engaging with these texts, chaplains can deepen their understanding of the theological principles that underpin their work and enhance their practice in diverse and dynamic contexts.

PROFESSIONAL STANDARDS AND GUIDELINES FOR CHAPLAINCY PRACTICE

Professional standards and guidelines are essential for ensuring that chaplains provide high-quality, ethical, and effective spiritual care. These standards and guidelines help to define the scope of chaplaincy practice, establish expectations for professional behavior, and provide a framework for continuous improvement. This appendix outlines key professional standards and guidelines for chaplaincy practice, drawing on the policies of leading chaplaincy organizations.

Code of Ethics

Respect for Diversity

1. Inclusion and Respect: Chaplains must respect the diverse cultural, religious, and personal backgrounds of the individuals they serve. They should provide care that is inclusive and sensitive to the unique needs of each person.

Reference: Galatians 3:28 (ESV) - "There is neither Jew nor Greek, there is neither slave nor free, there is no male and female, for you are all one in Christ Jesus."

2. Non-Discrimination: Chaplains must not discriminate based on race, ethnicity, gender, sexual orientation, religion, or any other characteristic. They should advocate for the rights and dignity of all individuals.

Confidentiality and Privacy

1. Confidentiality: Chaplains must maintain the confidentiality of all interactions with individuals, except in cases where disclosure is required by law or necessary to prevent harm.

Reference: Proverbs 11:13 (ESV) - "Whoever goes about slandering reveals secrets, but he who is trustworthy in spirit keeps a thing covered."

2. Informed Consent: Chaplains must inform individuals about the limits of confidentiality and obtain their consent before sharing any personal information.

Professional Integrity

1. Honesty and Transparency: Chaplains must be honest and transparent in their interactions, avoiding any form of deceit or misrepresentation.

Reference: 2 Corinthians 8:21 (ESV) - "For we aim at what is honorable not only in the Lord's sight but also in the sight of man."

2. Avoiding Conflicts of Interest: Chaplains must avoid conflicts of interest that could compromise their professional judgment or the care they provide.

Competence and Professional Development

1. Continuous Learning: Chaplains must engage in continuous professional development to maintain and enhance their skills and knowledge.

Reference: 2 Timothy 2:15 (ESV) - "Do your best to present yourself to God as one approved, a worker who has no need to be ashamed, rightly handling the word of truth."

2. Self-Awareness: Chaplains must engage in regular self-reflection and seek supervision or consultation when needed to ensure the quality of their care.

Ethical Decision-Making

1. Ethical Conduct: Chaplains must adhere to ethical principles in all aspects of their practice, making decisions that prioritize the well-being and dignity of those they serve.

Reference: Micah 6:8 (ESV) - "He has told you, O man, what is good; and what does the Lord require of you but to do justice, and to love kindness, and to walk humbly with your God?"

2. Consultation and Collaboration: Chaplains should seek consultation and collaborate with other professionals when faced with complex ethical dilemmas.

Standards of Practice

Spiritual Assessment and Care

1. Comprehensive Assessment: Chaplains must conduct comprehensive spiritual assessments to understand the spiritual needs and resources of individuals.

Reference: Proverbs 20:5 (ESV) - "The purpose in a man's heart is like deep water, but a man of understanding will draw it out."

2. Individualized Care Plans: Based on the assessment, chaplains should develop individualized care plans that address the specific spiritual needs of each person.

Interdisciplinary Collaboration

1. Team Collaboration: Chaplains should actively collaborate with other professionals to provide holistic care that addresses the physical, emotional, and spiritual needs of individuals.

Reference: Ecclesiastes 4:9-10 (ESV) - "Two are better than one, because they have a good reward for their toil. For if they fall, one will lift up his fellow."

2. Communication: Chaplains should maintain open and effective communication with other members of the care team to ensure coordinated and integrated care.

Crisis Intervention and Support

1. Immediate Response: Chaplains must be prepared to respond immediately to crises, providing emotional and spiritual support to individuals in distress.

Reference: Psalm 46:1 (ESV) - "God is our refuge and strength, a very present help in trouble."

2. Crisis Management: Chaplains should have skills in crisis management and de-escalation to stabilize situations and provide appropriate interventions.

Documentation and Record Keeping

1. Accurate Documentation: Chaplains must maintain accurate and timely documentation of their interactions and interventions, following organizational policies and standards.

Reference: Habakkuk 2:2 (ESV) - "And the Lord answered me: 'Write the vision; make it plain on tablets, so he may run who reads it.'"

2. Confidential Records: All records must be stored securely and accessed only by authorized personnel to protect the privacy and confidentiality of individuals.

Professional Relationships

1. Boundaries: Chaplains must maintain appropriate professional boundaries with individuals to avoid dual relationships and ensure ethical conduct.

Reference: Proverbs 4:23 (ESV) - "Keep your heart with all vigilance, for from it flow the springs of life."

2. Respect and Empathy: Chaplains should demonstrate respect and empathy in all interactions, fostering trust and rapport with those they serve.

Guidelines for Professional Development

Continuing Education

1. Educational Opportunities: Chaplains should pursue continuing education opportunities, including workshops, conferences, and online courses, to stay updated on best practices and emerging trends.

Reference: Proverbs 18:15 (ESV) - "An intelligent heart acquires knowledge, and the ear of the wise seeks knowledge."

2. Specialization: Chaplains are encouraged to seek specialized training in areas such as palliative care, mental health, and interfaith ministry to enhance their expertise.

Reflective Practice and Supervision

1. Reflective Practice: Chaplains should engage in regular reflective practice to evaluate their experiences,

identify areas for improvement, and enhance their self-awareness.

Reference: Psalm 139:23-24 (ESV) - "Search me, O God, and know my heart! Try me and know my thoughts! And see if there be any grievous way in me, and lead me in the way everlasting."

2. Supervision: Regular supervision and peer consultation are essential for providing support, guidance, and accountability in chaplaincy practice.

Certification and Credentialing

1. Professional Certification: Chaplains are encouraged to obtain certification from recognized professional organizations to validate their skills and knowledge.

Reference: 1 Timothy 4:14 (ESV) - "Do not neglect the gift you have, which was given you by prophecy when the council of elders laid their hands on you."

2. Credentialing Requirements: Chaplains should stay informed about and meet the credentialing requirements of their specific field and organization.

These professional standards and guidelines provide a framework for ethical and effective chaplaincy practice. By adhering to these principles, chaplains can ensure they provide high-quality spiritual care that respects the dignity and diversity of those they serve. Continuous professional development, ethical conduct, and collaboration with other professionals are essential for maintaining the integrity and impact of chaplaincy services.

347

www.ingramcontent.com/pod-product-compliance
Lightning Source LLC
Chambersburg PA
CBHW071920150726
47999CB00001B/44